The Valley of the Dry Bones

The Conditions That Face Black People in America Today

Rudolphf R. Windsor

Illustrated by El Hagahn

Windsor's Golden Series
P. O. Box 310393
Atlanta, Georgia 30331

First Edition 1986

Reprinted 1988 by Windsor Golden Series

Third Printing, 1990
Fourth Printing, 1991
Fifth Printing, 1992
Sixth Printing, 1993
Seventh Printing, 1994
Eighth Printing, 1996
Ninth Printing, 1998
Tenth Printing, 1999
Eleventh Printing, 2000
Twelfth Printing, 2001
Thirteenth Printing, 2002
Fourteenth Printing, 2003
Fifteenth Printing, 2004
Sixteenth Printing, 2006

Manufactured in the United State of America
ISBN: 0-9620881-0-2

Library of Congress Catalog Card No: 83-90249

Contents

Preface

For many years, I have analyzed and reflected on the profound problems of the black people in America and the problems of mankind in general. I believe that there are definitive reasons for the plight of the black people. I maintain that the sufferings of the black people did not happen by accident, but are the direct result of the violation of universal divine laws, "and until black people study and correct these violations, then and only then can we extricate ourselves from the cesspool of social destruction." He that does not learn from his mistakes is doomed to repeat them.

I strongly advise the reader to read my first book, titled *From Babylon to Timbuktu*. This book is a history of the ancient black races, including the black Hebrew Israelites. By reading my first book, the reader can acquire a background knowledge of many important points discussed in this, my second book.

It behooves me to express my appreciation to the faculty of Gratz College and Temple University, who taught me much, although it was the knowledge of my remote and recent ancestors and their affiliation with the Marcus Garvey movement that gave me the key to the true understanding of black history. Without this key to understanding, the established educational institutions would have brainwashed me into a state of confusion and deception.

Moreover, I want to express special thanks to the black teachers and rabbis (Able Respes) and my family: mother,

Leatta Jones; wife, Mary; uncle, Stanley Clark; brother, Cole
Windsor; and cousin, Zipporah Clark, for their patience and
understanding.

The Valley of
the Dry Bones

1

Economic, Social, and Political Problems of Afro-Americans

Introduction

With the many problems confronting the black people in America, the economic problem is probably foremost in importance, because it concerns survival (meeting the bill payments). Later in this book, I shall deal with the social and political behavior of the black people in America. In chapter 3, I shall convey my reasons why I believe the black man is trapped in a state of terrible social decay; afterward, I shall give my solutions to our manifold problems. In the meantime, I shall analyze, first of all, the negative behavior of the Afro-Americans in the economic sector.

Because of the increasing rate of unemployment among Afro-Americans, especially the youth, and the rapid immigration of Orientals (Koreans, Laotians, and Vietnamese) to America, it behooves me to explain some of the reasons black people do not own more businesses and have a higher rate of employment.

The black people in this country don't control more businesses because of their false orientation and negative thinking. (As a man thinkest, so is he.) Gradually, after many

1

years, I have experienced and learned that events and things in this world just don't happen by accident, but are caused by man, who is under the influence of the Universal Divine Presence. Where there is an action or deed, there will be, sooner or later, a reaction; this is universal law. For example, if you plant a seed in fertile soil and it gets proper rain and sunshine, the reaction is germination (growth). If you beat a child constantly without demonstrating love, the reaction will be fear or hostility. After the black man had been torn away from the umbilical cord of mother Africa, brought to America, and divested of his true history, culture, and language, some of the black leaders directed and steered the black masses toward the road of assimilation and extreme integration in every hostile aspect of American life, rather than directing the black people to construct their own thriving communities and businesses.

The psychological reaction to this kind of leadership took shape like a maniacal fever. Integration meant (for blacks) uniting with the white race in politics, businesses, and social entertainment, but black people had no bargaining power. "White was right"—it was the best and no less, people thought. The integration mania grew in such great proportions that black people, unaware of their glorious history, believed that to be black or dark-skinned meant to be inferior. The saying from 1900 through the late 1950s was "if you are black, get back." Aside from the Moorish American, some Muslims, Garveyites, and the black Hebrew Israelites, most black Americans believed in integration at any price, even at the cost of their lives at hands of the Ku Klux Klan. To most black people, integration meant riding in the front seats of trains and buses, eating and sleeping in white restaurants and hotels, going to white theaters and movies, and working in any and all kinds of white businesses in order to be around white people, with the purpose of dating and sleeping with them. With this kind of self-hatred and integration fever spreading like wildfire,

the reactions of the black masses were obvious. They thought, *We don't want to establish any black businesses; we only want to work in the white ones and advance up into white society.* Many years ago, I overheard a black man saying, "If we establish black businesses, we shall be segregating ourselves." This is the fundamental reason why so few black people have businesses in America. However, there are also other reasons.

The second reason that there aren't many black businesses is that there is no tradition—the passing down of the businesses from father to son—like you find among other groups. For example, the Italians have Giodano and Sons, the Jewish people have Levin and Sons, and the Irish have Daugherty and Sons. This is not to say that some blacks don't hand their businesses down to their children, but in proportion to other ethnic groups, blacks don't have many businesses to hand down. Another reason is that blacks are conditioned to the work hours of nine to five and, in the beginning, to be successful, most small businesses must be open for at least twelve to sixteen hours. In addition, many small businesses don't require a lot of money, but require a reinvestment of the profits—that is a turning over of the money you make back into the business. Many people can not afford to do this, especially if they have to hire help and have many other expenses. In this case, family support is necessary. Lastly, many blacks do not enter the business world, because they feel that it is a white man's domain or the domain of other ethnic groups.

The Attitude of Black Customers toward Black Businesses

The attitude of many black customers toward black businesses is negative in various manners. Many of us are familiar with the crab complex or crab attitude; this expression originated from the nature of the crabs in a barrel. If one crab

3

will make an attempt to get out of the barrel, the other crabs will invariably pull him back into the barrel. The crab attitude manifests itself in many ways among black people, and it can be defined as any negative, unhelpful behavior in which a particular race of people work against each other, especially when the members of the race have common problems inherent to the entire group—for example, racism, unemployment, a low ratio of education, high crime rates, and so forth. Like the crabs that have a common problem of being enclosed in a barrel, nevertheless, they will work against one another and pull each other down. Likewise is the behavior of hundreds of thousands of black people in America.

Some time ago, I had a bad experience with a woman who acted like a crab. I had a refreshment cart, which I pushed around the streets. After I had made a complete circuit of the neighborhood, it was my practice to wait fifteen or twenty minutes on a certain busy corner to serve my customers.

When I was starting to make another circuit of the neighborhood, a certain woman, a known bigmouth, yelled out to me, "Hey, mister, we don't want you selling around here; we are trying to keep someone from opening a store on the corner!"

I said, "I am not a store; I am a vendor."

The woman asked, "Do you have a license? Show me your license!" I replied angrily, "I don't have to show you my license." (As a matter of fact, I had the license, but I was only obligated to surrender it to the police or the agent from the Department of License and Inspection.)

She said vehemently, "If you don't show me your license I will call the police. "

I exclaimed, "Call the police!" Then I asked her, "What are you interested in the most—prohibiting me from selling around here or seeing my license?"

She did not answer me, so I went on my way. About a

half-hour later, while I was selling my refreshments, a police-man drove up alongside of me and requested to see my license. I showed it to him, and he read it and said, "You are all right; continue on with your business."

If you are like me, you can probably conjecture what the white police officer thought and said to his relatives and friends.

Let us pretend for a moment that the police officer is attending a party and one of his friends approaches him and asks, "How are things going in the police department, Joe?"

Joe answered, "Everything is pretty good. The other day, they transferred me to an all-black neighborhood, and I am learning a lot about black people that I didn't know before but had only heard about."

"What do you mean, Joe?"

"Well, yesterday I received a call about a man selling on the streets without a license. After investigating the situation, I found out that the man had a license. You see, many people complain that black men are lazy and don't want to work, and yet when one found a job and tried to make an honest living, without stealing, one of his own kind reported him to the police. I just don't understand these n——rs; they are against their own kind, and they have a nerve to talk about white folks."

Many black people have their own personal stories that they can tell about the crab complex.

There are many other negative attitudes that black people have toward black business people; some are understandable, and others are not. First of all, many blacks believe that a black man or woman should not be in business; many believe that this is a white man's domain. Moreover, they look at another black businessperson as if to say, "You should not be in business" or "How in the hell did you manage to get into business?" Some say that a black man's prices are too high, but they never say the price of alcoholic drinks is too high.

5

In addition, when you reduce your prices some say the prices are too low and think that something is wrong with your products.

When I was in the fruit-and-vegetable business, I sold tangerines, twenty for one dollar. Once a lady said to me, "Twenty for a dollar? How can you sell them twenty for a dollar? What is wrong with your tangerines that you are selling them so cheap?"

"Nothing," I said. "If you don't want twenty for a dollar, I'll sell you ten for a dollar."

This story proves that you cannot satisfy everybody all the time. Now, let me explain more about high prices.

Most black business people have to charge more for their products, because they simply pay more; any small-businessman, whether he or she be black, white, or yellow, has to charge more, especially if he is black. The black businessman does not belong to an association. Therefore, he can't buy his products collectively and obtain a greater discount or bypass the wholesaler altogether. If the black public wants greater employment and more black businesses, they will have to bear more of the burden of high prices from some black business people. This is a sacrifice that we must bear for the benefit of the entire community. This is not asking too much, because many black people, in the first place, are "penny wise and pound foolish." This saying is derived from the English monetary system, in which a pound is something like a dollar. So the cliché above refers to a person who endeavors to save a little and, on the other hand, is foolish, because he spends or wastes a lot. When a black person is financially able to buy from a black business and refuses to do so, but buys from a supermarket to save ninety-nine cents and, after that, goes to the seashore or on any type of vacation and spends anywhere from five-hundred to five-thousand dollars, he is pound foolish. Moreover, if a person goes to a supermarket rather than a

black business and then goes to the liquor store or the bar and spends anywhere from two dollars up to two-hundred dollars, he is foolish and pound foolish, with no racial pride or principles.

The Lack of Black Business Results in the Destruction of The Black Community. How So?

The lack of black business results in a higher rate of unemployment, especially among males and youths, leaving thousands of black males idle, standing on the corners cursing, drinking, shooting craps and scheming to commit crime. As a result of unemployment, the crime rate skyrockets. Empty stores become burglarized by the unemployed men; the decent, stable people in the community move out, but before they can sell their homes, the dwellings are vandalized by the unemployed and the dope addicts, who seek to sell what they have stolen in order to satisfy a seventy-five-dollar-a-day habit. Of course, the price of dope is set by the kingpins of organized crime syndicates who saturate the neighborhoods with the poison that destroys all communities and particularly the black ones. Blacks rip each other off by saying, "A nigger ain't shit," bringing down the esteem and self-image of a people trodden underfoot for generations. Those unemployed become poor family supporters; the basic unit of society, the family, is broken up. The black woman becomes tired of her unemployed man or husband. She does not need him anymore. She is either working or on welfare and does not respect the black male anymore. She can get all she wants from the system, which caters to the woman. The system gives her a job quicker than her man. If she is not working, she gets food stamps, money, medical assistance, and a grant for college. All she

7

needs is a baby or two or an apartment, and the state will not be late with assistance.

This kind of behavior in the black community, the crime, the vandalizing, the dope traffic, the self-hatred, the breakup of the family, causes division in the black community. There is a class struggle and a sex struggle in the black community: The stable and financially secure blacks are against the dire hard-core and abject poor. The men and woman are against each other. The women cannot respect the men. The root cause of most of these problems is the unemployed black male who displays a bad image in the community. Many of these unemployed burglarize what few black stores there are, forcing them to close up in disgust. This kind of situation produces self-contempt among black people and leaves a vacant store available for members of other nationalities to occupy.

The Eurasian Invasion of the Black Community

The word Eurasian means European-Asian (a person that is of these two bloods). However, here I mean the influx of Europeans and Asians into the black ghetto. In this section, I shall examine the impact that the other ethnic groups, particularly the Orientals, are making among the black people, especially in the larger cities.

In recent years, the black community has had a rapid influx of Orientals, including Koreans and Vietnamese. Most of these Orientals have settled in the large cities, and some have settled in smaller towns across America. Some Orientals, as well as other immigrants, are told to open up businesses in the black community; they are told what to sell, what black people like to eat. It seems as if there are Koreans on every corner, and in between the corners, you find more Koreans, Greeks, and the new immigrant Italians. In the city of Philadel-

phia, you find a new pizza shop franchise. These Italians came into the black community a short time ago. Some of them can't speak English but have become our lords and masters. They collect our money and give us steak sandwiches and pizzas. We work hard all week, the few of us who are employed, then often wait in long lines to be served by Europeans. We sometimes accept insults from them that we would not accept from another black person, and yet we continue to take our money to them, like docile lambs. These immigrant businessmen make us feel as if they are our lords and masters, like Genghis Khan, the pharaohs, and the Caesars of ancient Rome, and we are their subjects.

We give homage to them. In which way is this true? We, as a race, allow them to establish stores in our areas. We watch them do it and do nothing about it. We go bowing unto our lords, taking them baskets full of our money; we are happy to take it to them, because we recognize that we are weak, and they are strong. We respect and honor them. If this weren't true, we would not patronize them. We say in our hearts, *Mr. White Man and Mr. Yellow Man, you can have my money. But a n——r's teeth may grit, but none of my money shall he get.*

Most foreigners ought to be grateful to the black people, because we employ tens of thousands of foreigners and at the same time unemploy ourselves. Can a people be so stupid? Yes! When a people are brainwashed, they can be incredibly stupid. We employ foreigners in this manner: After the aliens have established businesses in our communities, we the un-employed (blacks have the highest unemployment rate) take our money to them, making jobs available for the fathers, mothers, sisters, brothers, sons, daughters, and friends. By taking our business to them, we are keeping them employed and keeping ourselves unemployed; it is as simple as that. The aliens take the money that we give them and help their own race. They take our money to help newer immigrants to

expand their businesses. The Italians give to the Italian business association; the Koreans give to the Korean association, and so on. You can't blame any race for helping their own. This is what God wants each race and family to do: Help your own kind first, then help others later. Black people had better learn to do this as quickly as possible, before it is too late. Time is running out.

The aliens use the money they get from our patronage to buy $75,000 homes and wall-to-wall carpeting (while most of us inherit wall-to-wall roaches); they use our money to send their children to college and to private schools in the suburbs, and our children have to remain in the inferior schools of the ghetto; they use our money to take three weeks' vacation in Rome, Berlin, Paris, Seoul, Tokyo, or Hong Kong, and most of us are lucky if we can get out of the dirty ghetto at all. In short, the aliens in a very short period of time rise higher and higher up the social ladder, and most of the blacks get lower and lower. Our money does not circulate in the black community; it immediately goes out of our community and benefits the people that discriminate against us and do not work for our fundamental interest. The answer to our prodigious problem will be rendered in later chapters, but for now, suffice it to say the benefits for the establishment of black enterprise outweigh the disadvantages.

In the beginning, the price of patronizing black businesses will be high, in some cases. However, in the long run it will be beneficial to the black community as a whole. How so? 1. It will create jobs; black businesses and jobs will engender more self-esteem and respect for one another. 2. It will remove the blight from the community. 3. It will make the black economically self-sufficient. 4. The problem of job discrimination will be reduced. 5. Black businesses will have the ability to retain the professionals and people of high standards in the community, which is necessary for a good image and revitalization of the black community.

10

The Black Political Struggle after the Civil War

Background

The principle issues that led to the secession of the Southern states and the Civil War were states' rights, the tariff, slavery, and the struggle between the Democrats and the Republicans for control of Congress. During the period between 1790–1860, the Democrats controlled the federal government for fifty years out of seventy. During this period, the Democratic party was the party of the slaveholders. Abraham Lincoln's Republican party freed the slaves and began to give them civil rights.

Perhaps, it is more proper to say that the blacks freed themselves with the help of God. The Civil War started in 1861, and in the early stages of the war, the Union army suffered several major defeats; the second battle of Bull Run was a major Union disaster. Defeats like this one motivated Lincoln and others to recruit blacks into military service, a move that, up to this time, the men in power had resisted. The industrial might of the North and the flower of white manhood could not alone win the Civil War for the Union of the United States! This fact is confirmed by Abraham Lincoln himself. When requested in the year 1864 to give up the use of black soldiers, Lincoln declared, "Take from us and give to the enemy the hundred and thirty, forty, or fifty thousand colored persons now serving us as soldiers, seamen, and laborers, and we cannot longer maintain the contest [the war]."[1] History demonstrates that most wars fought by the United States could not have been won, except with the help of God functioning through the unwavering loyalty and supreme sacrifice of the black man. After contributing his body, sweat, toil, tears, souls, minds, and blood for the development and security of this nation, the black man has still not acquired complete social and civil rights, but is slapped in the face

11

every day. The trends indicate that he is on the verge of losing some of the civil rights he has gained. I shall deal with this point more fully later in this chapter.

The Transitional Objectives

After the defeat of the slaveholders during the Civil War, the main objective of the federal government under the leadership of the Republican party can be outlined as follows: (1) the formation of a huge relief bureau to support the immediate needs of the ex-slaves; (2) the confiscation of the lands of the slaveholders and their transmission to the blacks and poor whites; (3) the deliverance of complete political, social, and economic rights to poor whites; and (4) the reorganization of the political climate of the defeated southern states in such a way as to guarantee political domination by the blacks and the poor white masses and to make it impossible for the return of political power to the ex-slaveholders.

The Hypocrisy of Andrew Johnson and the Northern Democrats

Before the blood had dried completely on the battlefield, evil forces of the Democratic party in the North and the South had united and were at work trying to undermine and preclude any black political control in the South! The chief leader of these Democrats was President Andrew Johnson himself.

Johnson was a Southerner, having been born in North Caroline. He moved to the state of Tennessee, where he held quite a few political offices. By the time the Civil War began, he had already served in the House of Representatives and

had been elected to the United State Senate. When the South seceded from the Union, the Southern politicians walked out of the Senate, and Johnson was the only Southerner to remain there. When Lincoln became president, he appointed Johnson military governor of Tennessee. When President Lincoln ran for a second term, the Republican party drafted Andrew Johnson as Lincoln's vice-president. Lincoln and Johnson won the election on the Republican ticket, but Johnson never became a Republican. Finally, Lincoln was assassinated on April 14, 1865, and Johnson became the Democratic president, although he had been elected on the Republican ticket.

When Johnson became president of the United States, he immediately said, "Treachery must be made infamous, and traitors must be punished and impoverished." This statement led many, especially the radical Republicans, Charles Sumner, Thaddeus Stevens, and others, to believe that Johnson intended to deal harshly with the Rebels; punishing the Rebels was the precise intention of the radical Republicans. But Johnson's harsh statement on the Rebels was nothing but a smoke screen to conceal his true desire (the restoration of the ex-slaveholders to power) and to throw his opposition in Congress off guard. Time has proven this fact to be true. Moreover, his subsequent deeds and actions testified against him and against the Democratic party north and south of the Mason-Dixon line.

Within three months, President Johnson came into conflict with Congress; he made a complete about-face, asserting that the Southern states had never been out of the Union, that the power to reconstruct the South belonged to the President and not to Congress, and that there must be lenient terms for the rebelling states.

Just six weeks after the assassination of Lincoln, on May 29, 1865, President Johnson issued his Amnesty Proclamation, which said, "All persons who had participated directly or indi-

rectly in the rebellion, save certain groups, would have all their rights and properties (except the ownership of slaves) restored to them upon taking a loyalty pledge." Those not pardoned included Confederate government officials of the South; or those that deserted from military, judiciary, congressional, and civilian posts; or those who had brutalized black soldiers; or those who had an annual income of $20,000 or more who had been involved in the rebellion. This list only included a relatively small group of Rebels.[2]

Although Johnson's proclamation stated that Confederate officials would not be pardoned, he gave many of them an indirect pardon. This was achieved in this manner: Many of the top officials of the South were never brought to trial, including Jefferson Davis, president of the Confederacy, and Alexander Stephens, the vice-president.

In retrospect, it is obvious that Johnson and his supporters intended to reduce the black man to a status of semislavery, which became known later as peonage or sharecropping, and to pardon the ex-slaveholders so that they could hold public office in the South and Congressional seats. Johnson sought to keep the black man in a state of semislavery by returning the big plantations to the planters, instead of dividing up the plantations and distributing them to the black man, forty acres and a mule; this dire situation kept the black man destitute, landless, weak, with no place to go but to remain on the plantations, living under the hostile yoke of the same slavemasters, to be exploited to the highest degree. Again, Johnson pardoned the Rebels in order to enable the ex-slaveholders to sit in local, state, and federal governments, rendering them political power over the helpless blacks.

After Andrew Johnson established all-white state governments in the South (although 4 million blacks lived in these states), the white Southerners enacted "Black Codes." Because of the stringency of these laws, many Northerners believed

that their aims were to keep the black man in a status of involuntary servitude, if not actual slavery. Blacks could not function as preachers without a license. They were not permitted to carry firearms. The blacks could not serve on juries, nor could they vote. They were denied the choice of approaching whites unasked and they could not own land. Any white man, rich or poor, could arrest a black man. Severe work rules were enacted. Black laborers became known as servants, irrespective of sex or whether they worked indoors or outside; and the employers were known as "masters." Employers could flog a laborer under eighteen years old and older laborers by the mandate of a judge. For the violation of working sites before the termination of their contracts they could be arrested and all costs charged against them. In the spring and summer, they worked from twelve to sixteen hours a day.

When slavery was abolished and the Civil War came to an end, the freemen left the plantations to look for work in other places and to find scattered members of their families. New regulations sought to discourage this movement. Blacks were required to go to sleep at an early hour. Laborers who were missing from their jobs were fined; the amount was double their wages. If anyone ran away from his work, he could be arrested and hired out to other master-employers. This was the beginning of the horrible peonage-sharecropping system in the South. The concept was to bind the black man to the plantations like an inmate in a penal institution, as was accomplished under slavery.

When Congress convened in December of 1865, the vast majority of the Senators and Congressmen from the rebellious Southern states stood in the halls of Congress to appeal for their seats. The audacity of the ex-slavemasters is manifested by the fact that the new representative of the notorious South were four Confederate generals, six Confederate cabinet officers, five colonels, fifty-eight Confederate Congressmen, and

Alexander Stephens, the vice-president of the Confederacy. Although President Johnson had organized the South, became its chief benefactor, and brought Southerners to the doors of Congress, his power ended here; only Congress itself had the authority to admit new representatives.

The Northern bourgeoisie and the radical Republicans were confronted with a serious problem. There was a possibility that the ex-rebels would again get control of Congress with their Democratic allies in the North, and this was a continuation of the prewar contest for power between the masters and the industrialists of the North and a tremendous reinforced Democratic party. The radical Republicans reasoned that if the Johnson scheme was allowed to proceed without a challenge, the entire Civil War would have been in vain. At this time, two prominent Republicans stood up and spoke out for true democracy and for the black man.

The Emergence of Black Political Strength in the South

There were two important Republicans who initiated legislation in Congress that made it possible for black men and poor whites to gain civil rights, Charles Sumner and Thaddeus Stevens. In early December of 1865, the Republican caucus met and devised a reconstruction plan for the Southern states. Basically, it constituted four stages: (1) asserting that the entire issue of reconstruction was the perogative of Congress; (2) considering the moves taken by the president as only temporary; (3) asking the House and the Senate to suspend action on the consideration of the acceptance of the Rebels from the South; and (4) to choose a committee of fifteen

from both houses of Congress to enquire into the state of affairs of the Rebel states.

The aforementioned reconstruction program was ratified by both houses of Congress, and it postponed indefinitely the seating of the Southern Rebels. As I had mentioned earlier, this move was highly necessary in order to preclude a Southern Rebel Democratic bloc from standing in the way of civil-rights legislation. With the rebel representation bared from Congress, it was possible for a predominantly Republican Congress to establish the Freemen Bureau and to enact and pass the Thirteenth, Fourteenth, and Fifteenth Amendments to the Constitution.

The Freemen Bureau was established in 1865, and it brought stability to the lives of the freed slaves. At that time, 4 million slaves had been released from slavery at once, creating a serious social and refugee problem. Many were destitute; they did not own land; they were illiterate; and they did not have jobs, food, or medical attention. The bureau established hospitals, supervised work contracts, interpreted laws, fed the hungry freemen, made sure that blacks got justice in court, and used the U.S. Army to maintain order in the hostile South. The head of the bureau, General Howard, estimated that the bureau handled a minimum of 100,000 complaints yearly. "At times," he said, "one was inclined to believe that the whole white population was engaged in a war of extermination against the blacks."[3]

The Union League, Carpetbaggers, and Scalawags

The Union League, in cooperation with the Freemen Bureau, made great progress in organizing and educating the freemen and poor whites in the political process. The political

area was all new to the freemen, and they needed a lot of knowledge and experience in order to compete with the hostile white society. These leagues were located all over the South, and the majority of the black people belonged to them. When the meetings were being held, the black people would stop their work to attend. The Union League was getting so strong that the ex-slavemasters made many attempts to break them up. As a result, many blacks had to arm themselves.

In the process of the reestablishment of state governments in the South, the black man had important allies in his rise to political power. First, these were masses of poor whites and, second, a large group of Northerners. These Northerners had come south with the Union Army and remained; other were officials of the Freemen Bureau or some other social agency. The ex-slavemasters termed these two groups "scalawags" and "carpetbaggers." The word *carpetbaggers* was derived from the fact that these Northerners came South, often with all their belongings in carpetbags. The word *scalawag* is derived from the Shetland Islands, north of Scotland, and was first applied to an undersized inferior pony. In light of this, when the old aristocracy of the South called the lower-ranking whites by the name "Scalawag," they meant worthless or inferior people; moreover, both carpetbaggers and scalawags were Republicans.

Black Political Personalities

With the coalition and assistance of the scalawags and carpetbaggers, the blacks were able to build up a powerful Republican political machine in the South. Naturally, all of this could not have been possible without the passage of the Fourteenth and Fifteenth Amendments (which gave to the black man citizenship and the right to vote) and the aid of the

18

Freemen Bureau, the Union League, the U.S. Army, and the Northern blacks who came to the South to help their brothers and sisters. As a result of this assistance, many blacks were elected to public office.

When the Civil War ended, there were 5 million whites and 4 million blacks in the South. Out of these numbers, 700,000 blacks and 660,000 whites were registered to vote at the beginning of the Reconstruction Period. Almost 200,000 whites could not register to vote or hold public office, because of their participation in the rebellion. Pertaining to the number of registered black and white voters, these were large figures, considering the fact that eighteen-year-olds and women could not vote in those years.

As a result of the political organization of the new freemen, many blacks were elected to various public offices. Examples were the mayor of Natchez, Mississippi, Robert Wood and W. Cuney, who ran for mayor of Galveston, Texas. There were hundreds of black elected officials in the state legislatures of the Deep South. In South Carolina, there were eighty-four blacks in the first Reconstruction legislature. In the cities and towns, there were black judges and sheriffs.

The state of Virginia sent one black congressman to Washington; Georgia sent one; Alabama sent three; North Carolina sent four; Florida sent one; Louisiana sent one; Mississippi sent one; South Carolina sent eight. Some of these states had black superintendents of education, major generals, Speakers of the House of Representatives, associate justices of state supreme courts, secretaries, treasurers, and lieutenant governors, and there were two United State Senators from the state of Mississippi, Hiram Revels and Blanche Bruce.

Mississippi had one black lieutenant governor, South Carolina had two, and Louisiana had three. Lieutenant Governor P.B.S. Pinchback became governor for forty-three days upon the impeachment of the previous governor. Although

19

blacks held many offices in the South, they never elected any U.S. senators from South Carolina, even though they had a superiority of over 100,000 in population; furthermore, the blacks had a population majority or a registered-voter majority in South Carolina, Mississippi, Alabama, Florida, and Louisiana, but not once did these states elect a black governor. This was a sad state of affairs. Let us examine the social and psychological behavior of white and black people during the post–Civil War period in order to arrive at a reason why there were no black governors in these states.

The blacks did not elect any black governors, because some had fear in their hearts. Some thought that the office was a white man's domain; some thought that whites had more brains; some felt obligated to the carpetbaggers and scalawags; and others thought that they had to conciliate and pacify the whites. The senator from Mississippi, Hiram Revels, a black man, spent so much time conciliating hostile, deceptive white people that he alienated black people. This even happens today. Some blacks spend so much time in white society that the masses of the black people don't even consider them black anymore.

Also, the white man used a psychological tool known as the "power of suggestion." When the state convention met in South Carolina during this period, white men indicated to the blacks that it would be more diplomatic to elect a white chairman. This is tantamount to saying that only a white man could do the job. It is psycho-social brainwashing. The power of suggestion is employed in our mass media today, in newspapers and on radio and television. It is so pervasive in our society that it would require a separate book to deal with that subject. Psychological suggestion in the mass media is a form of brainwashing. As a result, the black people are more a victim to it, because they may read fewer books and watch and listen

to the sound boxes more than other groups.

After the black man received his voting rights in 1868, it was the general feeling among whites that the black man should do the voting and the white the directing. What they meant was that the whites would rule and hold the dominant positions. The whites took a paternalistic attitude toward the blacks; as a result, some blacks believed that they should take a backseat or side seat and not offend the sensibilities of the whites.

We have a case in point when the state convention met to nominate a governor in Louisiana during this period. The black politician, Pinchback, took a backseat and withdrew his name from nomination, thinking that it would be unwise to have a black governor the first time. This is one of the mistakes he made. He later regretted it, and blacks suffered from it in future years. After Pinchback withdrew his name, there were two names remaining in nomination, those of Warmoth, a white man, and Dumas, a black man. There was a tie between these two on the first ballot. Most of the delegates were black and previous slaves and did not like ex-slaveholders. Before the next ballot was cast, Warmoth stressed the fact that his opponent (Dumas) had owned slaves. When the ballot was cast and counted again, Warmoth won by two votes.

The second mistake made here was that the black delegates did not forgive their own black brothers; they should have elected Dumas, the lesser of the two evils. Because they did not, they missed their chance to have a black governor. Finally, by the time Pinchback decided to run for governor in later years, the whites had gotten complete control of the election machinery.[4]

"Those who do not learn from history are doomed to repeat it." This is why blacks have repetitive setbacks, because they don't learn from history. Some say, "I don't want to learn

about that old slavery stuff" or "I am not an African; I am an American." But most blacks are not treated like Americans, but as less than Americans.

Although we did not have any black governors, nevertheless, we had a larger number of black elected officials in the South during the Reconstruction period than we have today. With this fact in mind, do you think we really advanced? The black politicians and their white allies changed many of the outdated inhuman and discriminatory laws that were on the books for many years in the Old South.

These black-white state legislatures enacted better, more equitable, and more humane laws for everybody. Some of the highlights of these laws were the establishment of public schools (under the old traditions, blacks and poor whites were excluded from schooling); general manhood suffrage, the granting of rights to females (such as divorce and the right to hold property), equity of civil rights, and a system of assistance to senior citizens. They abolished the old slave laws, penal incarceration for debt, the use of sitting in stocks and the whipping posts, and property requirements for voting. Under the old slave system, the masses of the poor whites who did not own property were prohibited from voting. Also, under the new system, the masses of the poor whites and the blacks who did not own property were now considered in state representation according to their mere population rather than by the ownership of property. At this time, I don't want to fail to mention the fact that these legislatures established social-service institutions for the orphans, blind, disabled, and insane. As you can see, these were reforms of extensive magnitude. It was no wonder that the big plantation owners and other racist writers hated the black–poor white coalition in the state governments of the South. In later decades, the struggle for social and labor rights developed into a fight between the rich and the poor, and the rich used the idealogy of white supremacy to divide the poor-white workers and the

blacks. (There will be more on this subject later.)

A seeming plus came to the black people when Congress passed the Civil Rights Bill of 1875, which gave blacks the right to equal treatment in hotels, public conveyances, and theaters and other places of public amusement. Possessing a sizable amount of political power in the states of the Deep South, the blacks were moving up and riding high in the saddle. What was the general mood and the social life of blacks, at least on the higher level? The great writer Lerone Bennett, Jr., gives us a classic example:

> Negroes and whites were going to school together, riding on streetcars together and cohabiting, in and out of wedlock. (Negro men were marrying white women in the South, but it was more fashionable, investigators reported, for white men to marry Negro women.) An interracial board was running the University of South Carolina, where a Negro professor, Richard T. Greener, was teaching white and black youth metaphysics and logic.
>
> A man, in his age, went to mail a letter and the postmaster was black. A man committed a crime, and in some counties was arrested by a black policeman, prosecuted by a black solicitor, weighed by a black and white jury, and sentenced by a black judge. It was enough to drive some men mad; it was enough to warp some men's judgement. Come with James S. Pike, a northern reporter, into the South Carolina House of Representatives, the first Western assembly of its kind with a black majority. "The Speaker," Pike reports, is black, the clerk is black, the doorkeepers are black, the little pages are black, the chairman of the Ways and Means (committee) is black and the chaplain is coal black.[5]

But this social atmosphere did not last long in the South. The forces of counterrevolution and reaction of the ex-slaveholders were at work undermining and eroding, slowly but surely, the foundation of black social, political, and civil rights all over

the South. Intimidation and mass murder became the order of the day, and gradually the black man was deprived of all his civil rights. By the 1880s, the state governments in the Deep South had returned to the complete control of the plantation owners.

How and Why the Ex-Slaveholders Seized Power

Before we involve ourselves in the heart of the issues that contributed to the seizure of political power by the plantation owners in the South, I want to list some of the inherent misfortunes and mistakes that were made as early as 1865 and onward. They were as follows: the pardoning of the Rebels by President Andrew Johnson; the restoration of the property (plantations) of the Rebels; the disarming of the black troops (while Rebels were permitted to keep their arms); the breakup of the Anti-slavery Society in 1870 (it should have been converted into the Anti–Jim Crow Society); the formation of the Ku Klux Klan in 1865; and the deaths of the two magnanimous white civil-right fighters Thaddeus Stevens and Charles Sumner, who both sat in Congress and died in 1868 and 1874, respectively. These misfortunes and mistakes were the foundation of doom and facilitated the rapid political decline of the black man and made him an easy victim of superexploitation.

Land

In 1862, during the Civil War, the federal government issued the Confiscation Act; this act empowered the president to seize the plantations of the Rebels, and it was generally understood that the enormous estates would be divided up and distributed to the poor whites and the ex-slaves. Con-

gressman Stevens unsuccessfully tried to get Congress to adopt a land-distribution policy. Distribution of land taken from the big landowners was not an unusual thing; during the French revolution, the new government seized the land and distributed it to the common people. Moreover, 400 million acres of land were confiscated from the landowners after the Russian revolution and handed to the people.

The federal government never transferred large amount of land to the millions of freed slaves in the South. Why? There is an extremely important reason for this, which we will explore shortly. After the Civil War, General Sherman gave large tracts of land to the blacks on Sea Islands, off the coast of South Carolina, with government approval. But the government welshed on its promise; it pardoned the Rebels and returned their land. The real government land policy was demonstrated in 1865 with the establishment of the Freemen Bureau. Federal policy at that time stated that the bureau could rent land to the freeman. However, with the restoration of the land to the Rebels, this provision proved to be of little benefit to the freemen.

The government had a number of options they could have taken. In 1862, the Congress passed the Homestead Act. It could have opened up large areas in the West and Northwest for the freemen, but they failed to do it. Why? If whites could not tolerate blacks in their own midst, they could have sent the blacks to the "ice box" of Alaska, yet they failed to do this. Why? Frederick Douglass proposed to the government that it set aside $1 million so that the freemen could buy land at easy terms; they failed to do this. Why? The government gave 23 million acres of land to the railroads, but had none for the ex-slaves. Why? There were large tracts of land that the government never restored to the Rebels because of the nonpayment of taxes. In fact, speculators, not freemen, got most of this land. Why?

In order to understand why the government vacillated

and refused to grant land to millions of poor whites and blacks in the South, or anywhere else for that matter, it is indispensable that we know the development of the labor movement in America. It is an established fact that the industrialists, capitalists, and big bankers control this country and many other countries. The big politicians are not free agents; many industrialists, interest groups, and bankers control the politicians. This fact holds true today, as it did over one hundred years ago. The writer and labor leader Terrence Powderly tells us that "When the workingmen were enlisting in the service of their country the bankers and owners of gold were working their way into Congress. . . . .A speaker on the floor of the House of Representatives said, after looking around him, 'I see the representatives of eighty banks sitting as members of this house.' "[6] The speaker said this during the Civil War. William Foster reveals to us that the Whig party, the forerunner of the Republican party, was dominated by Northern capitalist groups in alliance with slaveholders of the South. Now, read this, the same writer tells us that the "pro-slavery Democratic Party was controlled by the southern planters in alliance with Northern banking and commercial interests."[7] It is a fact that many Northerners profited from the slave trade and the exploitation of the blacks and poor whites in the South. It was the Northern bankers and commercial interests who constructed the ships that brought the slaves to America; it was these same Northern commercial interests that manufactured the chains, fetters, and shackles that bound the hands and feet of the slaves. The plantation owners shipped much of the cotton, sugar, tobacco, and other raw materials produced by slave labor, to the North to be manufactured. History and research shows that the Democratic party in the South and the North amassed great wealth from the institution of slavery.

These Northern commercial magnates ran for office in the US Congress or backed other politicians who supported

their business interests. In the South, many slaveholders held important offices in the House and Senate of the United States; one such slaveholder was Senator Jefferson Davis, of Mississippi, who owned a 10,000-acre plantation and hundreds of slaves. Holding high positions in the government from the presidency on down, these Democrats in the north and the South made the abolition of slavery very difficult. The power of the Democratic party was finally broken when the Democratic South seceded from the United States and became the Confederate States after 1861. The newly formed Republican party, the party of Lincoln, became the dominant party during the Civil War and the Reconstruction Period (1861–1880).

What did the Republican party gain from the war? (1) The control of the federal government; (2) the building up of stronger industries in the North; (3) an increase in tariff against foreign competition, which also permitted Northern industrialists access to Southern raw materials; (4) the Northern capitalists' moving into the South to begin the process of industrialization; and (5) the Northern Capitalists' gaining of poor whites and blacks as political allies. With the political support of the workers, farmers, middle class, poor whites, and blacks, the Republican party was able to win the national elections of 1868 and 1872 and the close elections of 1876 and 1880.

The Diabolical Republican Double Cross of the Black Man

During the Republican administrations, they abolished slavery and gave the black man citizenship and the right to vote. In 1875, they even passed a civil-rights bill that permitted black people to ride in public conveyances and to enter hotels, inns, and public amusements. Because of the liberality of the

Republican party, blacks were zealously dedicated to the Republicans; they voted the Republican ticket with a religious fervor. Mr. Bennett and Mr. Foster tell us that any black in those days who voted the Democratic ticket was treated like a traitor. (By the way, black people did not become diehard Democrats until the Franklin D. Roosevelt administration.) The records reveal that black registration and voting exceeded 85 percent in the Republican party. After the national elections of 1872 and 1876, the Republican party showed less and less interest in the enforcement of civil rights; they abandoned the black man to the whims of his archenemies, the wizards of the invisible empire of the Ku Klux Klan. How and why did this happen?

The Election Sellout of 1877

The two principal candidates in the national election of 1876 were Samuel Tilden, a New York Democrat and Rutherford Hayes, a Republican from Ohio. Two main public issues militated against the Republican party were the economic crisis of 1873 and the graft scandals; in spite of this, the Republicans stressed the insurrection of the Democrats during the war and their terror through the Reconstruction Period. The Democrats campaigned for "full autonomy for the South"; this meant the restoration of complete power to the plantation owners and their descendants. The election was a close one.

According to the final Republican count, Hayes received 4,033,768 votes and Tilden 4,285,992, with a plurality for the Democratic Tilden of 252,224 for the popular vote. Now, when the electoral votes were counted, Tilden received 203 against Hayes' 166. The Republicans contested the election returns from four states, South Carolina, Louisiana, Oregon, and

Florida; no doubt, there was widespread fraud in the South, with the mechanism of terror employed to keep blacks away from the polls. The Republican challenge left the undisputed votes at 184 for Tilden and 166 for Hayes. That was one vote lacking for Tilden in the electoral college, leaving the results in four states in dispute.

In order to resolve this critical problem, Congress formed a federal commission consisting of five Senators, five Congressmen and five Supreme Court justices. On the commission were seven Democrats and eight Republicans. The commission counted, recounted, and questioned the returns from the disputed states.

The crisis dragged on for three months; the excitement, tension, and suspense got higher. The Democrats filibustered in Congress in order to interrupt the orderly counting. Some Democrats called for an army of 100,000 to march on Washington to install Tilden in office. There were other Democrats who thought that if they could delay things until Inauguration Day, the nation would be without a president and on the verge of another civil war. The capitalists wanted to get back to normal business. The politicians rushed back and forward to secret rooms, exclaiming "Compromise, compromise!"

There can be no compromise without both sides surrendering something. The capitalist Republicans surrendered the black people as a sacrifice on the burning altar of the South. The Republican Hayes agreed that if the Democrats would not challenge the decision of the commission (the Republicans had the majority) the Republicans would permit the Democrats to take control of the two remaining Republican states in the South, South Carolina and Louisiana, the Democrats could have "states rights," and Hayes, upon taking office, would withdraw federal troops from the South.[8] The crux of the sellout was giving the South the freedom and right to put the black man in "his place." This meant in a semislave condition,

to be exploited politically, socially, and economically, with the North looking the other way. The subjugation of the black man was easily accomplished, because in general, he owned no property, no homes, and had no place to go but to remain in a state of dependency on the hostile plantations. The federal government never gave land to the black man, because it was the intention of the Republican industrialists who control Congress to keep the black man landless and weak in order to participate in his superexploitation—for example, by working him long hours at low wages. This way, the rich got richer, a hundred times over, and the poor got poorer in this wicked sharecropping society.

Workers in Rebellion

Another reason for the Hayes betrayal of 1877 was the fact that the old political coalition of the Republican party was breaking up at the termination of the war. In the North, new political alignments took place.

The Northern aristocrats after the war realized the existence of a threatening phalanx of adamant new adversaries—the middle class, farmers, and workers—in an uprising against the cruel industrialist exploitation. These labor movements began to take shape in the West and the North.

The workers began to organize trade unions and to develop political action against their previous allies, the greedy capitalists. During the twenty-to-thirty-year period after the Civil War, they executed the most bitter strikes in America. The middle class in the Northern cities began to direct the battleline against the big trust companies, which were hurting the little manufacturers and small businessmen. Also, the farmer began to battle the high stipulations of the railroads and bankers. Within ten years, these upheavals began to operate in the South.

Phillip Foner describes the conditions among the industrial states: "Militant strikes, unemployment demonstrations and the growth of independent political action heralded the fact that the class struggle was sharpening. Frightened by the popular upheaval, the masters of capital began to look with favor at the prospect of an alliance with reactionary elements (racists) in the South. Together they could build a solid front against the people movement. Assured by the Southern conservatives that the status of the tariff, the national banks, and the national debt would not be disturbed, Northern capitalists no longer hesitated."[9]

It was this fear of the unification of the labor masses of the North with the poor whites and black masses of the South that motivated the Northern industrialist (Republicans) and Hayes to ally themselves with the white racists and to betray the black man in 1877. William Foster says: "In this raw deal, Hayes never consulted the leaders of the Negro people. He considered the Negroes, who were loyal supporters of the Republican Party, to be strictly expendable and he proceeded on that basis. It was a cold-blooded sellout that was to cause boundless misery and hardships to the Negro people and gravely handicap the fight for American democracy over many decades."

For seventy-five years, an all-out struggle for supremacy existed between the Southern planters and the Northern industrialist. This struggle climaxed in the Civil War and the terrible period thereafter. From 1801–1876, slavery or the black issue was the main national political question of both the Democratic and Republican parties. Mr. Hayes's deal of 1877 drastically transformed this state of affairs by mutually terminating the open fight between the planters and industrialists; as a result, it relegated the black question into a lesser position as a national political issue.[10] The black people began, once more, to influence national politics. This new influence was attributed to the fact that a large proportion of the black

population of the South had migrated to the North, where they were permitted to vote.

After the Hayes sellout, the Northern capitalists began to employ in their interest both the Republican and Democratic parties. These two parties became Northern capitalist parties. It did not matter which one won the elections; the Northern capitalist concerns were protected.

The Humiliation of Frederick Douglass

Frederick Douglass became the most important orator and leader of the black people from 1850 to 1875. He worked relentlessly for the abolition of slavery, editing several newspapers. Furthermore, he traveled extensively throughout America, speaking on behalf of his people and the Republican party, which had done so much for the benefit of the ex-slaves. It appears that, in light of the growing labor troubles in the North and the West and the new political alignment of the industrialists with the Southern planters, Douglass failed to understand and to deal properly with these new political changes. Consequently, he was unable to indicate the next fighting line or strategy for the black people. In retrospect, it seems that as the Republican party became less useful to the black man, Douglass should have urged the black people to support the new Populist party, which was a rapidly growing party of workers and farmers in the North and the West and had begun to move into the South. This party was the new alternative.

It seemed to me that Douglass had suffered from a condition of confusion, deception, and transformation shock. Some writers say that he did not speak out at the crucial time against the Hayes sellout. Because of the change of attitude

of the Republican party, Douglass seems to have been in a state of shock and disbelief. Undoubtely, he was confused on the proper course of action to take, considering the fact that the Democratic party was worse than the Republican. Then, worst of all, Douglass became a victim of deception; Hayes, the very man that sold out the black people, maneuvered Douglass into a position of neutrality by appointing him United States marshal in Washington, D.C. This appointment and his future appointments, as recorder of deeds and minister to Haiti, rendered Douglass ineffective as a strategist for the civil-right struggles.

Hayes humiliated Douglass by even offering him such an insignificant position. Douglass was a brilliant man of international stature; he had traveled to Europe and had discussions with Presidents Lincoln, Johnson, and Grant. Moreover, Hayes had had the nerve to offer him a job as a policeman when other black men were sitting in the state legislatures and in the Congress of the United States. Are black people so blind as to accept on one hand few crumbs and lose, on the other hand, all the accumulated advantages won through blood, sweat, and tears? This is just what happened to Frederick Douglass.

Mr. Douglass should have known better. There was earlier evidence that the system did not want black people to sit to the left or right hand of power. Back in 1863, Douglas had visited Lincoln and plans had been designed to place Douglass in charge of the recruitment of black soldiers. He had met with Secretary of War, Stanton. Believing that everything had been arranged, Douglass closed down his newspaper and prepared to assume his new assignment. However, Mr. Stanton reneged on his promise, because the position was too prestigious for him to place a black man in such an important assignment.[11]

During Johnson's and Grant's administrations, recom-

mendations had been made to appoint Douglass head of the Freemen's Bureau and to assign him to the post of minister to the black nation of Haiti in the Caribbean Sea, but these plans never materialized during these administrations.

The Second Civil War

Real terroristic war existed in the South from 1865–1925. Although the federal government of the United States officially ended the Civil War in 1865, the South waged another Civil War of political-economic repression, intimidation, and murder against the black man. After the Hayes sellout, he withdrew the federal troops from the South. This deliberate act gave the white racists a "free hand" to finish the final phase of the complete suppression of the black people. Here are listed some events and facts that indicate that virtual Civil War existed:

(1)   Secret Confederate Army personnel were organized by the Confederate general Forest; his secret army units were called the Ku Klux Klan (1865).

(2)   A national conference of the Ku Klux Klan met in Nashville, Tennessee, in 1867.

(3)   There were three race riots in Louisiana between September and October of 1868.

(4)   Governor Holden proclaimed a state of rebellion in parts of North Carolina in 1870.

(5)   On March 6, 1871, a race riot took place in Meridian, Mississippi.

(6)   Whites massacred more than sixty-five blacks at Grant Parish, Louisiana, in 1873.

(7)   Ku Klux Klansmen took sixteen blacks from a jail in Tennessee and shot them in 1874.

(8) In a race riot in Vicksburg, Mississippi, thirty-five blacks were killed in 1874.

(9) The governor of Mississippi declared martial law after rioters killed several black political representatives in 1874.

(10) More than ten blacks were killed in race riots in Yazoo City, Mississippi, in 1875.

(11) More than twenty blacks were killed in race riots in Clinton, Mississippi, in 1875.

(12) A request for federal troops to protect the rights of black voters in Mississippi was rejected in 1875.

(13) Five blacks were murdered in Hamburg, South Carolina, in 1876.

(14) The racial conflict got so bad that President Grant sent federal troops to Florida and South Carolina in 1876.

(15) All federal troops were withdrawn from the South to give the white racists a complete "free hand" to deal with the blacks in 1877.

(16) The traitor, President Hayes, appointed Frederick Douglas U.S. marshal for Washington, D.C., in 1877. This position rendered Douglass ineffective and was equal to making him a boy scout.

(17) Because of enonomic and political repression, blacks fled the South in 1879.

(18) In Danville, Virginia, a race riot broke out in 1884.

(19) More than eighteen blacks were killed in Carrollton, Mississippi, in 1886.

(20) Wilmington, North Carolina, was the place where eight blacks were killed in 1898.

(21) In New Orleans, whites burned a black school and thirty homes in 1900.

(22) The Supreme Court upheld the Alabama constitution, which disenfranchised blacks, in 1903.

(23) Martial law was proclaimed in Atlanta, Georgia, after ten blacks and two whites were killed in 1906.

(24) A race riot raged for five days in Springfield, Illinois.

(25) The Ku Klux Klan spread like wildfire in the South and the West. The estimated membership in 1915 was 4 million.

(26) Race riots took place in Philadelphia; four were killed. In Chester, Pensylvania, five were killed. Both events took place in 1918.

(27) The governor of Oklahoma said that a state of rebellion and insurrection existed because of the Klan activities; as a result of these activities, he proclaimed martial law in 1923.

(28) In Washington, D.C., 25,000 hooded Klansmen paraded to demonstrate their ideology and strength in 1925.

This is only a partial list of riots and murders committed against black people, and it does not include the individual cases of murders, which number in the thousands. Furthermore, I am aware of the fact that numerous race riots and murders transpired after the year 1925.

New Forms of Slavery

I mentioned earlier how the big Northern industries began to move into the South. Industries such as tobacco, lumber, textile, iron and coal mining, steel, and railroads began to increase. These industries were established under the control of Northern capital; Southerners did not have any great amounts of capital after the Civil War. Some of the big names of Northern monopolists who moved into the South

were Thomas Ryan, Jacob Schiff, and August Belmont. Another industrialist, J.P. Morgan, developed the Southern Railroad from the West Point Terminal Railroad. By 1908, Morgan had taken over the Tennessee Coal, Iron, and Railroad Company. Within a short time, other Northern industrialists had entered into coal, lumber, and other industries. By the turn of the century, these capitalists had invested about a billion dollars in the South and dominated its economy and politics.

With all of this Northern investment in the South, there was a great demand for cheap labor, and it was really found among the poor whites and the blacks. Aptheker reveals to us that the Northerners, in collaboration with the Southerners, subjected the blacks to the most brutal exploitation.[12] Perlo make this point clear about the Northern capitalists and the Southerners: "Their economic course was to prevent the Negro people from getting the land, to preserve the plantation system in a new set-up (sharecropping and chain-gang slavery) in which Northern bankers, merchants and manufacturers derived the lion's share of the profits from its operation, with the Southern landowners as junior partners and overseers."[13]This was the same system that operated during the slavery period. What we must understand is that sharecropping was slavery; they only changed the words and the legal explanations attached to them. The new masters of the South transformed the ex-slaves into half-free servants. As sharecropping became a form of slavery, which will be dealt with more in detail later; chain-gang labor also became a form of slavery.

The chain gangs were the wretched institutions of Southern society. They served two primary purposes: (1) They were disciplinary institutions formed to break the spirit of young black boys and men and to teach them to be docile. (2) Many young black men were arrested, convicted on the least excuse, then hired out to unscrupulous people and companies to be

worked in fields, camps, mines, and railroads from sunrise to sunset. Many companies made contracts with the local government to work these young blacks, and some amassed great wealth from chain gangs. Lerone Bennett gives descriptive details of chain-gang life: "With chains welded to their bodies, waist deep sometimes in mud and slime, convicts toiled day in and day out. Fortunes were founded on their misery. Their quarters were unbelievably filthy. Vermin, investigators reported, crawled over their clothes and their bodies. And it was not unusual for a female prisoner and a male prisoner to be chained to a bed at night. Fletcher Green, a modern scholar, concluded that they had no parallel except in the persecution of the Middle Ages and the concentration camps of Nazi Germany." [14] Don't some of these details sound familiar today, with the constant harassment and arrest of black youth (by the police) throughout America?

In one of a series of articles published in *The Philadelphia Tribune*, dated September 24, 1981, a former police officer, Stephen Henderson, said that while he was a member of the Philadelphia Police Department, he was frequently disturbed by the contempt many police officers (in particular, white officers) harbored against black youth in particular and black people in general. He said he knew of dozens of instances where black youths were targets of police abuse in the form of unnecessary or unwarranted arrests and beatings. Henderson said that it seemed as though the police want all black youths out here to have criminal records so that, in the future, they will surely never be able to get a job and thus be rendered useless to society. It seemed like the only place some forces in this society want black youths and black men is in jail.

Henderson said that he too was concerned with the apparent apathy that existed in the black community in relation to crime, especially crimes of blacks perpetrated upon blacks. He said that while the black community has readily acknowledged that "black-on-black" crime is a problem in the commu-

nity, it has left the responsibility for cleaning it up to the police, the district attorney's office, and social-service agencies. Henderson contends that if the black community allowed outside agencies to do the job that they could be doing in the home and in the community, then more and more black youths would fall by the wayside. He suggested that many of these youths could be saved, but would instead wind up on a conveyor belt that begins with petty crime and ends with a lifetime of criminal activity and incarceration.

The above article was written in great detail and was of considerable length; thus it is not appropriate to reprint the entire article. I must express my congratulations to the writer, Pamela Smith, for a job well done, and to the police officer, Stephen Henderson, for his knowledge and insight, and for his being magnanimous enough to place his name and reputation on the line so that the people could be better informed.

The Downward Trends

As you can see, the war continues against the black man, and it will more likely get worse before it gets better. The social decay of the black community today is worse than it has ever been, and the reasons are detailed in a later chapter. Many of the sociopolitical conditions and events that led to the persecution and loss of civil rights of the black people after 1875 are rehappening today. I shall list many of the similarities between the events after 1875–1880s and compare them with the events of the 1980s. My analysis demonstrates that the events between these two periods are similar:

(1) After 1875, there was no advocacy for the return to African culture that was necessary for the development of a strong black family and community, espe-

cially in a hostile environment. After 1975, the interest in black culture, history, and pride has declined tremendously.

(2) After the Civil War, assimilation and excessive integration became more important than the development of the black community. A similar situation exists today, and this is the reason there is a deterioration of the black community.

(3) Black ownership of business was far under 50 percent after 1875, and even today blacks don't own anywhere near 50 percent of the businesses in the black community.

(4) During the Reconstruction Period and thereafter, there was no powerful black middle class. The author William Foster said that if there had been, this middle class would have been able to successfully challenge the opposition of the racists during this period. Likewise, today there is no powerful black middle class that is indigenous to the black communities throughout America. I am not saying that a black middle class doesn't exist. What I am saying is that the majority of this black middle class derive their strength and status from the mainstream of white society rather than from black society. If this black middle class was fired from their jobs in white society, they would lose their middle-class status and be forced to join the ranks of the unemployed and the poor. However, if this black middle class owned and operated their own institutions and businesses in the black community, such as banks, insurance companies, supermarkets, clothing stores, hospitals, law offices, and so forth, they would become a powerful, indigenous black middle class, gaining their strength and status from the support of the black community. But this is not the case.

(5)   After 1875, some blacks spent a lot of time appeasing whites, and at the same time they alienated the masses of the blacks. (They lost the support of the blacks.) Today, the same thing is happening; some blacks play the role of "Uncle Tom," trying to satisfy the whites in order to enhance their own position. As a result, they become of no use to the masses of the black people. Some of these "Uncle Toms" are only leaders of the black elite and upper class, not leaders of the masses.

(6)   The black people, after 1875, put too much trust in the system and the Republican party. They should have placed their trust in the Creator God and in their own efforts. Today, we are repeating the same mistake, placing too much trust in the government. It is not what the government can do for us; it is what we can do for ourselves that is important. Excessive government handouts stifle human incentives. Many people are sitting around waiting for a check instead of building the black community. There is no other nationality that will clean up and build the black community; it must be accomplished by the black people.

(7)   At the end of the Reconstruction Period (1875), there was a great increase in Ku Klux Klan activity throughout the South and the West. Even in these modern times, the Klan has not only operated in the South, but has increased their recruitment and demonstrations in the North. Their primary target in the North has been the state of Massachusetts. Moreover, there has been mysterious deaths of black men all over this country; many are known to be racially connected.

(8)   Congress passed the General Amnesty Act in 1872, which pardoned most of the Rebels. Foster said this

"was interpreted all over the South as a sign of weakness and it did in fact indicate the new mood of conciliation growing in the Republican ranks." During the 1870s and 1880s, the Klan set the South in a state of turmoil. Some arrests were made, but the Klansmen were found not guilty. Just recently, in September, 1981, a jury found Klansmen not guilty of the murder of five men in Greensboro, South Carolina. These murders took place in November of 1980.

In recent years, the Philadelphia Police Department murdered at least three unarmed black men. Two had been handcuffed, then shot, and none of these three had committed a felony. When police officers were brought to trial for murder, they were found not guilty by practically all-white juries. In other words, they were pardoned for their crimes. Murders like these take place all over this nation every year. The conditions are definitely a repeat of the events that occurred after 1875.

(9) By the middle of the 1870s, conservatism was increasing in this country. The federal government showed less and less interest in the enforcement of civil rights; it withdrew from the South the federal troops that had protected the black people; the federal government left the enforcement of civil rights to the separate hostile Southern states, and, in 1883, the Supreme Court ruled that the Civil Rights Act of 1875, which had given black people equal treatment in public accomodations was unconstitutional. Now, many of the civil-right gains have been reversed and lost.

A rapid growth of conservatism is moving through America today, and President Reagan is the

leader of this movement. In 1876, President Hayes abolished the Freemen Bureau, which rendered social aid to the poor whites and blacks. In 1981, Reagan terminated many of the social programs from the national budget, with the support of a growing conservative Congress. Moreover, the Reagan administration has demonstrated less interest in civil rights. One example of this disinterest in civil rights is the statement expressed by Vice-President Bush at the governors' conference in Atlantic City, New Jersey, in the late summer of 1981. He said, "The Reagan administration will not enforce civil rights at the point of a bayonet." This statement means one or both of two things: (A.) The federal government will not use troops to enforce civil rights on the behalf of black people. (B.) The Reagan administration will not force civil rights on the individual states through the use of the courts. The trends and evidence indicate that the Reaganites have no intentions of prosecuting civil-rights violators.

The United States Justice Department completed a thorough investigation of the Philadelphia Police Department during the Carter Administration. This investigation revealed widespread civil-rights violations and police brutality against minorities, especially black people. The Justice Department under the Reagan administration never filed formal charges in court against the Philadelphia Police Department. The Reagan administration neglected to act; they let the August, 1981, deadline expire. Now it is too late to do anything about it. Was this an accident? Of course not! They are playing politics. The politicians in Philadelphia and in Washington have gotten their heads together behind

the scenes and have agreed to let the matter rest. This is how politics operates. Furthermore, we have not heard any vocal outcry in the black community demanding the Justice Department prosecute the police department just before the expiration of the filing date. President Reagan is not only cutting the budget, but he is also cutting the civil rights and throats of the black people. His inaction on civil rights sends a signal to the racists that they can murder black people with impunity. This is definitely a repeat of the events of 1876.

(10)   The goal of those evil men who hungered for political power in the South was stealing the voting rights from the black people. William Foster says: "This was done by sheer terrorism—the Negroes who dared to go to the polls did so at the risk of severe beating, if not at the cost of their lives. Besides, all sorts of trickery were used to disfranchise them." Buck paints this picture of the period:

Polling places were set up at points remote from colored communities. Ferries (boats) between the black districts and the voting booths went out of repair on election day. . . . In districts where the blacks greatly outnumbered the whites, election officials permitted members of the superior race to stuff the ballot box and manipulated the count without fear of censure. Fantastic gerrymanders (changing election districts) were devised to nullify Negro strength. The payment of poll taxes . . . was made a requirement for voting. Some states confused the ignorant by enacting multiple ballot box laws which required the voter to place correctly his votes for various candidates in eight or more separate boxes. The bolder members of the colored race met threats of violence and . . . physical punishment. When the black man succeeded in passing through this maze of restrictions and cast his vote there

was no assurance that it would be counted.

All of this happened after 1876 and the black man was deprived of the right to vote and hold public office. Signs indicating separate facilities for "whites and colored" people sprang up all over the South. After a short period of freedom, the black man had been reduced to a new kind of slavery; he became a prisoner once more in his own community, under the complete domination of his exploiters, without any recourse to justice. Carl Schurz, a German-American leader, revealed to us the Southern mentality that is still existent, to a great extent, throughout America today: "Men who are honorable in their dealings with their white neighbors will cheat a Negro without feeling a single twinge of their honor. To kill a Negro, they do not deem murder; to debauch a Negro, they do not consider robbery . . . they still have an ingrained feeling that the blacks at large belong to the whites at large."[15] The black man lived under these miserable conditions for almost a hundred years after Reconstruction and poured out his crying soul to God. He asked, "Why, O Lord, why has all of this trouble come upon us?" At the one hundredth anniversary of the end of the Civil War, Congress passed the Voting Rights Act, in 1965.

Congressman Gray of Philadelphia discloses that the act was significant: "In just one decade alone, black registration in the South nearly doubled." It is a known fact that throughout America the increase in black elected officials has tripled. At the time I am writing this, we have reached the year 1981 and the Voting Rights Acts of 1965 was in great danger. It was due to expire in August of 1982, and the conservatives in the Reagan administration and in Congress were seeking to kill it or dilute its power. However, the Congressional black caucus was seeking to extend the act another ten years. There are those who argue that the Voting Rights Act is not necessary. Congressman Gray said:

45

When I examined the statistics, I saw that in the act's sixteen-year existence, the Justice Department has objected to 816 proposed changes in the election laws of the 22 states covered by Section 5. I asked myself, if the act is no longer needed, why have fully 500 of these objections come in the past six years?

I also look at the testimony gathered by the House Subcommittee on Civil and Constitutional Rights. Its hearing found that in 1979, in one United States Senate race in the South, registered blacks found their names missing from the registration lists. Others were listed as deceased—quite prematurely. And polling booths were moved on election eve to undisclosed places.

Testimony before the subcommittee also showed that in Indianola, Mississippi, a city which was 80 percent black, the white city officials annexed suburban areas until white voters outnumbered blacks by three to one. Elsewhere, white employers drove blacks to the polls and told them how to vote. . . .

Furthermore, I have come to realize that whites of the South have indeed changed; many Southerners would still resurrect, given half a chance, the good ole days when cotton was King and Jim Crow was the sheriff.

All over the country the political system is trying to water down the political strength of black people. Recently in Philadelphia, Pennsylvania, the Honorable State Senator Milton Street used his dedicated efforts and influence to save the political seats of two of his fellow black lawmakers when the system attempted to reduce black political strength through the process of redistricting.

In order to reverse the social decay and the downward trend of the masses of the black people, there are a number of priorities and objectives that must be undertaken at once:

1. The black community must be organized on a

46

stronger cultural, familial, economic, and educational level.

2. The black community must organized in order to reduce black-on-black crime and syndicate-organized crime. The senior citizen, the young, males, females, and businesses must be protected. What hurts one hurts all, in the short or long run. It is a fact that the police cannot do the job by themselves.

3. When the Democratic and Republican parties do not serve our interest, the black community must support a third-party candidate.

4. Blacks must form political coalitions with other ethnic groups whenever it is beneficial to their interest.

5. The black community must organize to make it crystal clear to the politicians (black or white) that they cannot work against the interest of the people.

6. Blacks must vote out those politicians who are not committed to the people; they must be dedicated voters, or they shall lose the right to vote.

7. The black community cannot afford to set back in their rocking chairs and react only when a crisis develops; they must anticipate a crisis and move to confront it before it gets out of control. When black people refuse to vote, the system will conclude that they don't count; then they will not fear or consider us blacks. As a result, they will perpetrate anything against blacks and deliberately neglect to do the right thing for them. Remember that the poor, the uneducated, and the weak are easily exploited, so let us unite to prevent a return of the 1880s. If blacks don't unite and do this task well, then they are doomed to hell and shall have no one to blame but themselves.

We shall not unite under our blackness alone. With all our other common interests, we need to know something about our great culture and history; this knowledge will engender in us a feeling of racial pride to have the will and desire to cooperate in mutual projects for the improvement of the social welfare of the black community.

Many ethnic groups in America have utilized their history and culture as the foundation to accomplish racial pride and unity, and black people should learn to do the same. For example, the Chinese control their own communities (Chinatowns) with their cultural-historical traits: Chinese architecture, Chinese art, Chinese writing, Chinese food, Chinese dances, Chinese costumes, Chinese language, and Chinese holidays. This Chinese culture transmits racial pride to their people and plays a great part in uniting them to accomplish their goals. Moreover, black culture can accomplish the same thing for black people.

Notes

1. Carl Sandburg, *Abraham Lincoln. The War Years* (New York: Harcourt Brace Jovanovich, Inc.), V3:210.
2. Commoger, ed., *Documents of American History* (Englewood Cliffs, New Jersey: Prentice-Hall, Inc., 1974), V2:7–8.
3. Wilson, *The Rise and Fall of Slave Power in America* (New York: Penguin) V 3:501.
4. Lerone Bennett, Jr., *Before the Mayflower* (Books, Inc., 1966), 206–7.
5. Bennett, *Before the Mayflower*, p. 185.
6. Terence V. Powderly, *Thirty Years of Life and Labor, 1859–1889*, rev. ed. (Fairfield, New Jersey: Kelley, Augustus M., Pubs., 1940)58.
7. William Z. Foster, *The Negro People in America History* (New York: International Publishing Company, 1970), 147.
8. Allen, *Reconstruction*, 205–206.
9. Frederick Douglass, *The Life and Writings of Frederick Douglass*, ed. Phillip S. Foner (New York: International Publishing Company, 1975), 4.
10. William Z. Foster, *The Negro People in American History* (New York: International Publishing Company, 1970), 338 and 344.
11. Ibid., 276

12. Aptheker, *Jewish Life*..

13. Perlo, *American Imperialism*, 82.

14. Bennett, *Before the Mayflower, 1877–1913*, rev. ed. (New York: Pantheon Press, Inc., 1972), 239.

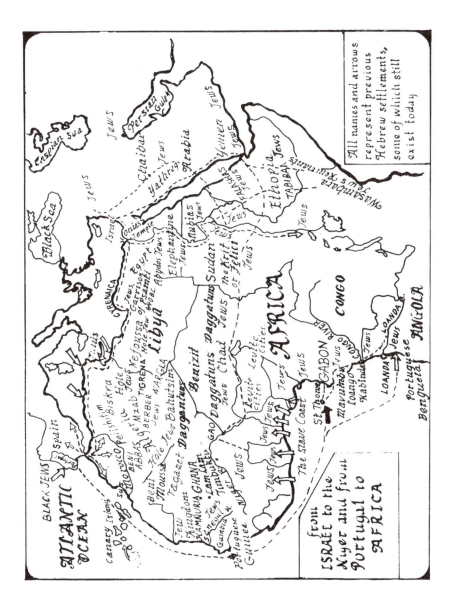

All names and arrows represent previous Hebrew settlements, some of which still exist today

from ISRAEL to the Niger and from Portugal to AFRICA

2

The Bible: An African Book

The Bible is an African book. Black people wrote the Bible, and they wrote it primarily about themselves, as I shall demonstrate. Then you can judge for yourselves. The first nation mentioned in the Bible is an African nation called Ethiopia (Genesis 2:13). The nation of Ethiopia mentioned here was part of the "Garden of Eden." Take notice that the African Hebrews did not mention anything about England, France, or Germany, but Ethiopia was the first nation mentioned. Just think of it. According to the white supremacists, the black people are supposed to be a people without a civilization, without a history, but yet the "Good Book" connects black people with the creation story and the first civilization. The Garden of Eden was located somewhere between Asia and Africa, where the Ethiopians dwelled. According to the European writer Max Heindel,[1] this garden was located on the sunken continent of Lemuria (east of Africa); this was where the first man and woman were created.

One of the ancient names for Ethiopia is Cush; this name is mentioned in Genesis 10:6–10. These Ethiopians lived not only in Africa but throughout the Middle East and Asia. Herbert Wendt,[2] the German writer, confirmed this point when he said "Asia was the cradle of the black race." The Hebrew scriptures related to us that the first great cities were constructed by the son of Cush, the great Nimrod. You can check

51

the word Cush in any good dictionary. it was these Cushites who built the great city of Babylon and other cities in Africa and Asia.

So far, we have seen that biblical scenes and stories took place in an African world and with African characters. Having African ancestors, the people were mostly black or brown. The land known as Palestine was called the land of Canaan in ancient times (Genesis 10:15–20); and the Canaanites were the blood brothers of the Cushites and Miyraimites (Egyptians)(Genesis 10:6). From the beginning, these African Canaanites lived in southern Turkey, Syria, Lebanon (then known as Sidon), Palestine, and Jordan. Ancient historians did not use names of continents, such as Asia or Africa; they used national or tribal names. Nevertheless, the African in the Middle East and the ones in Egypt, Ethiopia, and Kenya were descended from the same family. In light of this old information, Palestine and much of the Middle East would seem to be an extension of the African continent, just as Madagascar is part of Africa. We must not let European racists define history for us; they have made a terrible mess of it already. We must define history for ourselves and control our destiny. If we don't control our destiny, we shall always be controlled by others.

African People and Places

Another important point that proves that the Bible is an African book is the multiplicity of times that African places and people are mentioned, when compared to the times non-African people are mentioned.

The word *Rome* and its derivations are mentioned only twenty times in the Bible and not once in the Hebrew scriptures (the Old Testament), and the word *Greece* and its deri-

vations are mentioned only twenty-six times in the Bible and four times in the Old Testament. My conclusion is that these two European countries are used only four times in the entire Old Testament. This is next to nothing. Now, let us compare European words with African people and places used in the Bible.

The African city of Sidon and the Sidonians are mentioned more than 17 times, Ethiopia is mentioned 40 times, the African city of Tyre and the Tyrians are mentioned more than 57 times, the African people called the Canaanites are mentioned in the Bible, more than 153 times, and the Egyptians are mentioned more than 727 times. If you add up the number of times that African people and places are mentioned in the Bible, you will find that the references about African people exceed more than a thousand times—wow, that is incredible! If someone read a book and found in it information mostly about the German people, German culture, and German history and geography, we would have to conclude that the book was primarily a German book. Likewise, we find a plurality of information about African people and black people in the Bible: therefore, we must conclude that it is an African book.

When the writers of the Bible mentioned that the Hebrews Abraham, Isaac, Jacob, Joseph, and Moses went down into Egypt, this meant that they went into Africa. Egypt is in Africa. The Egyptians enslaved the Hebrew people for 400 years; these Hebrews were not Europeans, but African Hebrews. Moses, the Hebrew liberator and lawgiver, led his people out of the African nation of Egypt to the wilderness of Sinai (the peninsula east of Egypt). Like Palestine, Sinai is a part of Africa. The prophet Ezekiel knew this when he said, "Like as I (the Lord pleaded with your fathers in the wilderness of Egypt" (Ezekiel 20:36). The wilderness of the land of Egypt is the peninsula of Sinai; hence, it is part of Africa.

The Color of the Israelites

There is one question often asked of me: Were the ancient Israelites a white people in biblical days? The answer to this question is an absolute no. I have no doubt about my convictions and no reason to lie. The Europeans had the reason to lie: to develop white supremacy. They lied about the truth after they made it illegal for a black man to learn to read during slavery times; this event took place when the whites prevented the blacks from defending themselves. They reinforced their lie by placing white pictures throughout the Bible, placing white pictures on religious calendars, and producing lily-white television programs and religious movies. As a result of this insidious, overt deception, the modern generation (white and black) just assumes, without the facts, that the ancient Hebrews were white.

Does the Bible indicate, definitely, the color of the Hebrews? This question is important, because the Hebrews are the central figures upon whom the Bible is based. I maintain that Abraham, Isaac, Jacob, Ishmael (the father of the Arabs), Moses, Solomon, Jeremiah, Daniel, Jesus, and the entire nation of the Hebrews were a black people, and I shall give you proof to support my position. Some writers contend that the Hebrews were a white people, but they don't offer any proof. I think that it is a shame when a writer makes a statement, yet doesn't have enough respect for the reader to evince some proof. For most of my evidence, I shall cite the Bible. It is possible for me to render many other historical sources; however, since we are dealing with the Bible, the superlative proof should be the Bible. Let the Good Book speak for itself.

The Bible is a book that many read, but few understand or know the various races or their characteristics. Joseph was one of the twelve sons of Jacob. After he had been sold as a

slave to an Egyptian, he eventually became viceroy of the nation and was second to the pharaoh in authority. When a famine struck this part of the world, Jacob sent ten of his sons to the neighboring African country of Egypt to buy corn. Arriving in Egypt, the ten brothers came before Joseph. Joseph recognized his brothers, but they did not recognize him. (Genesis 42:1–8). Since the Egyptians were a black people, Joseph had to be black also. If he had been white, the ten brothers would have recognized him easily among black Egyptians.

At this time, the famine was so great in the Middle East that Jacob and all his children and grandchildren and their wives went into the African country of Egypt, (Genesis 46:26–28), and they dwelled there for over 400 years (Genesis 15:13 and Exodus 12:40). No white Jews were enslaved in Africa under black people at this time, only African Hebrews.

At this point, I would like to explain to the readers that Africa was the birthplace of the Hebrew nation; this birth was not in Europe nor in some remote place in Asia, but on the Nile River in Africa. In light of this information, I say to everyone who has been brainwashed that he should cease thinking that the original Hebrews were some color other than black. My reason for asserting that Mother Africa was the birthplace of the Hebrew nation is the fact that seventy persons went to Egypt (Exodus 1:5) and when they departed over 3,300 years ago, their number, excluding women and children, was 600,000. Sociologists know that there are always more women and children in a population, and when we count the women and children, we have over a million people. This was the Hebrew nation that was born in Mother Africa, a nation born in an African environment, born in an African culture, born in an African learning center, born speaking the Hebrew, African, and Egyptian languages. Moses was born here in

Africa as a Hebrew, but, reared as an Egyptian, he was educated among the royal family in one of the most advanced countries in the world.

After living in Africa for more than 400 years, the children of Israel went out of Egypt a mixed multitude (Exodus 12:38). The mixed multitude was caused by sexual relations between the Hebrew tribes and the Egyptian people. In addition, other African people who were living in Egypt joined the children of Israel in their struggle for freedom, and these Africans departed from Egypt with the people of Israel. When Moses instituted the Feast of the Passover in Egypt by the command of God, he had these other Africans in mind when he said the following: "And when a stranger shall sojourn with thee, and will keep the passover to the Lord, let all his males be circumcised" and "Thou shall neither vex a stranger" (Exodus 22:21 and 12:48) Yes, it is clear to our understanding that it was the Hebrews and other Africans (strangers, not born Hebrews) who were celebrating an African Hebrew feast (Passover) in an African country before it was celebrated anywhere else in the world. So we see that the first Hebrews were in Africa, and the Divine Creative Force first appeared to the Africans and to Moses in an African land and not in Europe. So, if you know your Bible and history, it should not seem strange to you that black Hebrews exist, because the first Hebrews were black and they developed as a people in Africa.

Do you need any more proof to be convinced that the Bible was written by Africans and that the ancient Israelites were a black people? I think that some of you do need more evidence, because you have been so strongly brainwashed by white-supremacy motion pictures like *The Ten Commandments* that some of you don't know that the nation of Egypt is in Africa.

The Curse of Leprosy

There are three kinds of leprosies mentioned in the Bible: (1) domestic leprosy, found in the houses; (2) material leprosy, found in garments; and (3) biological or physical leprosy, contracted by human beings. We are only concerned here with biological leprosy. As I mentioned in my first book, *From Babylon To Timbuktu,* pages twenty-four and twenty-five, the leprosy invariably stated in the Bible showed itself when the skin turns red, but mostly white. It is an established fact that the Bible always mentioned leprosy in the context of the skin turning white because of a disease or in relationship to some specific wrongdoings. If you don't believe that the ancient Israelites were black after I explain to you about the leprosy plague and curse, then you are either grossly stupid or you don't want to face reality because it disturbs your deepseated, fixed ideas that you don't want to change.

It is written in the thirteenth chapter of Leviticus: "When a man shall have in the skin of his flesh a rising, a scab, or bright spot and it be in the skin of his flesh like the plague of leprosy, then he shall be brought to Aaron the priest or to one of the sons of the priest."

And in the fourth verse: "If the bright spot be white in the skin of his flesh . . . the priest shall shut up him that has the plague seven days."

In the sixth verse we have "And the priest shall look on him again the seventh day: and, behold, if the plague be somewhat dark, and the plague spread not in the skin, the priest shall pronounce him clean: it is but a scab: and he shall wash his clothes and be clean."

In the second and fourth verses is mentioned a bright spot in the skin. (A "bright spot" means a lighter spot than the regular dark brown skin.) The explanation of the fourth verse is this: If the bright spot becomes white or whiter, then

the leprosy is spreading over the body. Remember Moses was speaking to the Israelites in the wilderness of Sinai, a part of northeast Africa.

Moses said in the sixth verse: "that when the priest shall look on him on the seventh day and behold the plague has become somewhat dark or darker and it did not spread then the priest shall pronounce him clean because the skin is getting darker like his regular or original skin."

Moses and Aaron in the thirty-eighth verse speak of bright spots and white spots. A black man or woman with these white spots covering some part of their body is a partial leper. However, once the plague of the whiteness has covered his entire body from his head to his feet, the leper is clean. He has completely changed color like the albino. The albino was once black, but his hair and skin have changed to white, and his eyes are pink. The people who had leprosy in the Bible are classified as albinos, and these albinos are the only white Hebrews that ever existed in ancient times and were in the minority.

The Bible never speaks of a white person turning black, but only of a black person turning white. Therefore, we can conclude that the black man was first on earth. Other places in the Bible where it is mentioned that the various people had turned white are Number 12:10 and II Kings 5:27. Leprosy is a disease caused by missdeeds (Deuteronomy 28:15 and 58–61).

Afro Hairstyles in the Bible

The great prophets of old gave us a clear indication of what the Israelites looked like in their days and what the messiah or great judge will look like in the future. John, the revelator, and Daniel, the prophet, described him as having hair like pure wool and wheels or feet like brass, as if they were burned in a furnace. The African man is born with woolly hair, and the man of African descent has feet like brass, as if

58

they were burnt in a furnace. The reader will note that I classify all black people, including black Hebrews, as people of African descent, just like all white people are of European descent, whether they live in the Americas, Asia, or South Africa.

Black people in the Bible are in the vast majority, not the minority; they are mentioned directly and indirectly. An example where they are mentioned indirectly would be in regards

The Afro-Asian Israelite

Most biblical personalities and Hebrews were black, like this man. Read Song of Solomon 1:5; Lamentations 4:8, 5:10; Job 30:30, and Ezekiel 1:7.

59

to leprosy (turning white). One example of a black person mentioned directly in the Bible is the woman speaking in the Songs of Solomon 1:5–6. She said, "I am black but comely, ye daughters of Jerusalem." The word *comely* means "beautiful," so, you see, the saying black and beautiful was fashionable and popular three thousand years ago, and it did not start first in the 1960s or 1970s. Because we had albinos among the ancient Hebrews, the intermarriages between the Hebrews and the Albinos produced every shade of color between white and black. These colors included high yellow, yellow, caramel color, brown, and dark brown.

"I am black but comely, oh ye daughters of Jerusalem. . . . Look not upon me because I am black because the sun has looked upon me [shone upon me]." Why did this young woman make this statement? Well, you see, the color of this woman was entirely black, and the color of the other women in King Solomon's chamber was brown. These were women that lived for the most part in the palace of Solomon. The woman that said, "I am black" was used to the outdoor life and taking care of the vineyard (Song of Solomon 1:6)— therefore darkened by the sun. Then she was brought into the king's chamber (Song of Solomon 1:4) as one of the women of Solomon. When the daughters of Jerusalem saw her, they snickered. As a result, the woman of the vineyard answered, "I am black but comely, oh ye daughters of Jerusalem."

The only person that can turn pure black must be black in the first place; a pure white person cannot turn black. He can turn red, then the skin will peel off and he will suffer great pain, because he does not have coloration or pigmentation in the skin. Now, let's see what other nationalities and other historical sources say about the color of the Hebrew Israelites.

A Roman historian named Tacitus, who lived about A.D. 90, said that many assert that the Jews are an Ethiopian race. J.A. Rogers commented that for the Romans to have

60

Top left: Two Falasha (Ethiopian Hebrew) families in Ashdod, Israel. Top right: Another Hebrew family in Israel. Bottom right: A Hebrew teacher and his wife in the Falasha village of Ambober, Ethiopia. (For other photographs of the Falashas, consult the *Encyclopedia Judaica*.) Bottom center: A Peul or Fula girl of West Africa. Experts say that the Fulas are of Hebrew ancestry. Bottom left: Some Hebrew Israelites from Angola, West Africa. (Friedrich Ratzel wrote about Israelites from Angola in his book, *The History of Mankind,* vol. 3, p. 134.)

considered them Ethiopians is a clear indication of their color, because the Ethiopians were black. [3]

The Moors from Africa ruled Spain and Portugal for about 700 years, and the Jews were in these countries even longer. When the Duchess L'Abrantes, the wife of Napoleon's ambassador to Portugal, was in that country, she commented that the Judeans and the Moors look alike. At this time, the Judeans were so dark that many whites thought that all Judeans were black.

King John II of Portugal deported many of his Judeans to West Africa (Angola), and many settled in the West Indies. John Bigelow, who went to Jamaica in 1850, saw the offspring of these Judeans and said that they were black. [4] The evidence show that the Judeans in Europe up to 1850 were virtually black but died out. As a result, the white servants of these blacks converted to Judaism and became the new Jews.

Color: It Doesn't Matter?

After convincing many black people that the ancient Israelites were a black people, some of them replied, "The color doesn't matter; it is the spirit of God that counts." Pertaining to this issue, I could not agree with them more, because God does not observe the color, but observes the deeds of man, and God will, indeed, judge those racists who distorted the truth. Those that say that "color does not matter"—don't tell it to me! Tell it to the white racists; convince them that color doesn't matter. They are the ones who lied about the black man's history in order to make blacks feel inferior and to make whites feel superior.

I don't need to deal with the terrible psychological damage the white race caused the black race when they instituted

slavery and discrimination. The color issue has cost many lives on slave ships, on the plantations, and in every city in America. It made the black man powerless, weak not only in his household but powerless socially, economically, intellectually, and politically as well; and since the color issue has done all of this, it does matter. If, by regaining a true knowledge of our history, we gain racial pride, self-esteem, a love of self, and a desire to cooperate with each other, this would be the first step toward the development of the Afro-American community.

The tentacles of the color issue have not passed away; they leave their recognizable scars over the world, even over the motherland of Africa. The wrong was set in motion centuries ago; this problem can only be corrected by revealing the truth and not by sweeping it under the rug. Every man should be given recognition for his individual worth and contributions, even about his true history.

The color issue is an injustice, and it does matter; any kind of injustice matters. If I murdered your relatives, would you say it didn't matter? If I rob and steal from you, are you going to say it does not matter? God forbid! If you say that the color issue does not matter (which is an injustice), are you Negroes willing to take the blame for all the wrongs committed against black people by white racists so that these racists, on the judgment day, may enter into paradise and you into hell?

It has been over 100 years since the abolition of slavery. Have you ever wondered why there are so few black doctors, policemen, lawyers, and engineers and so much disunity, so much illiteracy, so much unemployment, so much crime, so much distrust, so little racial pride, so few black businesses, and so many slums in black neighborhoods? The answer to these problem will be dealt with in this section.

Moses, the African Hebrew messiah and leader, prophesied to his African Hebrew brothers and sisters over

3,000 years ago. He reiterated to them the laws of the Universal Creator. Moses spoke to them like a father and warned them to keep God's laws, and if they would do them, he said, they would be "Blessed above all the nations of the earth" (Deuteronomy 28:1, In fourteen verses, Moses said that they would be blessed in health, agriculture, commerce, cattle industry, lending money, prestige, and victory in battle over their enemies.

On the other hand, Moses made it very explicit to his people that if they did not obey God's laws, which are conducive to an orderly society, free of crimes, then all these plagues, misfortunes, hardships, and curses shall happen to them until they change and do what is right (Deuteronomy 28:15).

Now, before I explain many of the details of the curses, it would behoove me to give you an idea of what the laws of God are. There are 613 Hebrew laws, which come under different categories; they are all found in the first five books of the Bible, which are called the five books of Moses. A brief summary of these laws would be the "Ten Commandments" found in Exodus 20:1 and the law that says "Thou shall love thy neighbor as thyself." Another way of saying the above is like this: "What is hateful to you, don't do to your fellowman," quoted by Hillel, an African Hebrew, in the first century B.C.

At this time, I shall proceed to explain in detail the curses and plagues that Moses predicted would happen to the African Hebrews if they should disobey the laws of God. These curses are in five categories: (1) the curse of worldwide dispersal, (2) biological curses (3) psychological curses, (4) economic curses, and (5) the curse of the loss of identity or nationality.

Notes

1. Max Heindel, *The Rosecrucian Cosmo-Conception* (Oceanside, California: The Rosecrucian Fellowship 1973), 277 and 304.
2. Herbert Wendt, *It Began in Babylon* (New York: Delta Dell Publishing Company., 1964), 368.

3. J.A. Rogers, *Nature Knows No Color Line* (New York: H.M. Rogers, 1952), 91, 123 and 130.

4. Bigelow, John, *Jamaica in Eighteen-hundred Fifty: The Effects on Sixteen years of Freedom on a Slave Colony* (Westport, Connecticut: Negro Universities Press).

A slave trader taking Hebrew-Israelite slaves more than 3,000 miles away from their homes. Read what the prophet Moses wrote in Deuteronomy 28:15, 32,34,41,45,48,49,64,65, and 66.

3

Curses

Worldwide Dispersal

Moses and many of the Hebrew prophets predicted worldwide dispersal, captivity, and slavery for the African Hebrews because of the violation of the laws of God. According to Deuteronomy 28:41, the Hebrew people would "beget sons and daughters, but they would go into captivity." It was the African Hebrew Israelite tribes who were taken by force from the West African coast and brought to South, Central, and North America as slaves. Once, I saw a movie about slave society: The slave woman had a very handsome son, whom she dearly loved. Then one day, she received word from her master that her son would be sold. She cried and pleaded with him, "Please, masa, don't sell my boy. I'll do anything, but don't sell my boy." The boy was sold anyway. The mother became hysterical and then depressed. Finally, she committed suicide by jumping into the Mississippi River. This is just one out of a thousand horrible stories like this. It is also written that "Thy sons and thy daughters would be given unto another people and thine eyes shall look and fail for the longing for them all the days long and it shall be no might in thy hands" (Deuteronomy 28:32).

It is written in Deuteronomy 28:64 that the Israelites would be "scattered among all people from one end of the earth to the other end." The African Hebrews were carried as slaves to Europe, Asia, North and South America, and even to the islands of the seas, such as the Canary Islands, Madeira,

the Cape Verde Islands, Madagascar, Guadeloupe, Saint Thomas, Guadeloupe, Martinique, the Virgin Islands, the Bahamas, Jamaica, and Cuba. (For information on the spreading of the black Israelites read the author's first book *From Babylon to Timbuktu*.

According to the predictions of the African Hebrew prophets, the original Israelites were to have gone into captivity and slavery (Deuteronomy 28:32, Lamentations 1:3, and Joel 1:3). The only people who were brought as slaves to the United States or to any other place in the western hemisphere were the African Hebrews. The rest of the Europeans came here as immigrants of their own free will; therefore, they do not fulfill Bible prophecy, nor do they qualify to be called the original Hebrews, but they can be converts to the Hebraic religion and culture.

Biological or Physical Curses

In addition to the Israelites' being carried away as slaves, the prophet Moses also predicted that a number of physical curses or plagues would consume the Israelites: "The Lord shall smite thee with a fever, and with a consumption [progressive wasting away of the body] and with a fever, and with an inflammation [a red burning open sore] and with extreme burning and with the sword, and with blasting [physical starvation] and with mildew and they shall pursue thee until thou perish" (Deuteronomy 28:22).

The worst episode of the life of a slave was the middle passage; this was the voyage from Africa to the Americas. The conditions on the slave ships were unbearable; two to four hundred slaves were packed like sardines in the bottom of the ships. Mr. Mannix, in his book *Black Cargo*, describes the plagues on slave ships: "Some wet and blowing weather

having occasion the porthold to be shut and the grating to be covered, fluxes and fevers among the negroes ensued. . . . The deck, that is the floor of their rooms, was so covered with blood and mucus which had proceeded from them in consequence of the flux that it resembled a slaughterhouse. . . . Numbers of the slaves having fainted they were carried upon deck where several of them died. . . ."[1]

"And the Lord will smite thee with the botch of Egypt, and with the emerods, and with the scab, and with the itch wherein those cannot be healed" (Deuteronomy 28:27). The botch of Egypt was a tumor or boil. The botch was one of the ten plagues that God brought up on the Egyptians by the hand of Moses (Exodus 9:9). Emerods are another name for boils; scabs are dried-up sores that protrude from the skin; the itch is a contagious eruption of the skin. The disease that they feared most on the slave ships was smallpox, because the doctors had no way of curing it until the end of the eighteenth century. If one man had it, he could infect a whole ship, unless he was thrown overboard the first time the scab appeared. Mr. Mannix tells us that Captain Wilson of the *Briton* lost more than half of his cargo of 375 slaves by not listening to his surgeon. They were loading on slaves, and the last one, said the surgeon, had signs of the smallpox. The captain did not want to part with this good slave, and within a short time many of the other slaves were infected with the disease. Henry Ellison said, "I have seen the platform one continued scab. We hauled up eight or ten slaves dead of the morning. Their flesh and skin peeled off their wrists when taken hold of being entirely mortified."

As the prophet Moses had predicted, the botch, itches, emerods, and scabs certainly infected these African Hebrews so that they could "not be healed."

Economic Curses

Cursed shall thou be in the city and cursed shall thou be in the field.

Deuteronomy 28:16

This prophecy applies to the period when the city of Jerusalem was besieged by the Babylonians, Greeks, and Romans. It refers to the extreme famine, disease, and destruction that ensued in this city. However, scholars are aware that there is duality and triplicity in prophecy. This prophecy applies to the life that Afro-Americans suffer in the cities of America and similar places. Just think of the plight in the black ghetto and you know what I mean. Our ancestors were not only cursed in the fields in Israel (because there was famine and no rain for the crops), but they were cursed in the fields in the South right after the Civil War. Many of the Afro-Americans worked as sharecroppers. The white landowners would supply the ex-slaves with food, clothing, tools, and other essentials, and the black sharecroppers would agree to work the land. At the end of the harvest, they would share the crops. Most of the time, the sharecropper did not have enough profit to pay for the landowners' advances of food, clothing, and tools. The sharecropper would work another year and find himself in deeper debt. If he tried to run away, he was fined and was sent back to the farm to work for less than a dollar a day to pay off the fine. This is not to even speak of paying off the debt. [2] Sharecropping was exploitation in the highest degree, because the Afro-Americans could not read most of the contract. The landowners deliberately took advantage of the sharecroppers by using devious means to require him to pay an outlandish percentage of the harvest, about two-thirds. This practice is like stealing the eyes from a blind man, then asking him if he could see.

"Cursed shall be thy basket and thy store" (Deuteronomy 28:17)—All the curses mentioned in Deuteronomy 28:16,

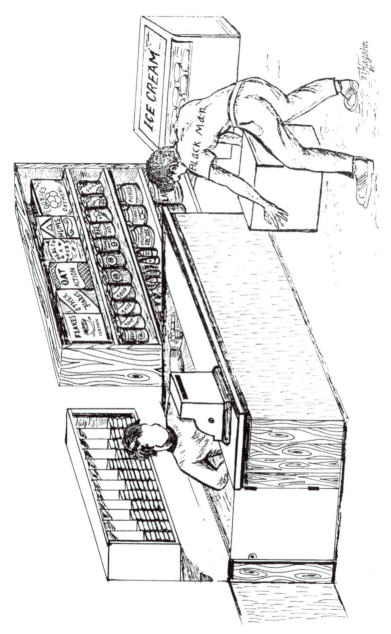

A black man working for a new immigrant who recently came into the black community. (Read Deuteronomy 28.)

71,18,24,38,39,40 talk about the crops in the field, fruit trees, vineyards, the land, and the flocks of sheep and cattle.

The above items refer to agriculture, commerce, the meat-packing industry, manufacturing, department stores, and supermarkets. According to the prophecy of Moses, the Afro-American is supposed to be cursed in all these enterprises. This is why Afro-Americans are not especially succesful in business. Remember Moses said, "Cursed shall be thy basket and cursed shall be thy store." "Thy basket" means the food supply and "thy store" means the retail stores and the warehouse where the food is stored. As I review all these curses with you in detail, you will see that they fit the black man in America and the western hemisphere more than anybody else in the world. By these cures and other historical facts, we know that the black people in this part of the world are the true Judeans or Hebrews.

"The stranger that is within thee shall get up above thee very high and thou shall come down very low" (Deuteronomy 28:43)—this forty-third verse is a very relevant prophecy for our day; it means that foreigners or other races that live in the same country or city as the African Hebrews will rise up the social ladder higher than the African Hebrews, and as a collective people, we find this very true from South America to North America. The African Hebrews have been in America since 1619, when the first bondmen (slaves) arrived at Jamestown, Virginia. Blacks have been in this country before many other races, fought in every war, built up this country, nursed and reared the slavemasters' children, and contributed to education and science. In every generation from 1619, we have seen new immigrants arriving in this country, and after one or two generations, they climb the social ladder, getting higher and higher above the African Hebrews who were born here. As a result, the African Hebrews, as a group, get lower and lower.

Now, we have reached the 1980s, and in the city of Philadelphia and elsewhere, there are many recent immigrants who acquired businesses in the black community. To take one example, the United States government has agreed to open the door to 12,000 Vietnamese refugees a month. Many black people complain about the high rate of unemployment in the black community, many complain that too many nonblacks are establishing businesses in black neighborhoods, but many blacks seem to be too weak and disorganized to do the same. They excuse themselves by saying, "The government must be subsidizing them." To be successful and blessed in business, we must keep God's law. To some people this might sound too puritanical, but divine law is necessary in order to live in an orderly society. But man does not want to live by God's law. God's law says thou shall not kill, thou shall not steal, thou shall not rob, love thy neighbor as thyself.

"Love thy neighbor as thyself"—the meaning of the Golden Rule is that you have to love yourself first, then your neighbor second. If you don't love yourself, you cannot love your neighbor. You must have self-esteem and racial pride first. After you have loved yourself first and have done for yourself, then you can begin to love your neighbor and to do something for him in a humanitarian sense. (Charity begins at home.)

To make it simple, in order to be blessed in business, we must love our neighbor as ourselves. Let us say that there is a vacant store in our neighborhood and some of the people would like to open a business but no one has enough money nor the collateral to borrow the money. So a few people decide that they will hold a community meeting. Let's assume that the community decides to open up a business and each week they decide to pool what money thay have. Now, doing this requires a lot of love, mutual respect, and trust. To put up your hard-earned money you must have love, to work for the

betterment of the neighborhood and to work for the good of others. "Thou shall love thy neighbor as thyself." When we set up this business, we can employ people. This improves property value, and we have an investment in the community of which we can be proud.

But, in order for this business to expand and be really prosperous, there are other laws of God we must obey. We must not steal nor rob from one another; we must not kill. If we contiinue to do these evil things, the curse will remain on us, because our brother will be forced out of business on account of the high crime rate. As a result, the stranger will acquire the same business and he will prosper.

"He [the stranger] shall lend to thee and thou shall not lend to him: he [the stranger] shall be the head, and thou shall be the tail" (Deuteronomy 28:44)—The stranger who just recently came to this country will prosper to a great degree in his new business; this will enable him to lend us money, but we will not be able to lend money to anybody else. Italians, Germans, Frenchmen, Irishmen, Poles, and others have climbed to the top of the social ladder, and the majority of blacks are still on the bottom of the socioeconomic scale; they are "the tail." Many of them are suffering from more curses than are written in this book; not only are recent strangers placed in the position to lend them money, but many of these strangers even deny blacks mortgage loans.

"Also every sickness and every plague which is not written in the book of this law, then will the Lord bring upon thee, until thou be destroyed" (Deuteronomy 28:61).

The Curse of the Loss of Identity

The word *identity* refers to a people's nationality, culture, history, and language; a people gets its nationality and language from the nation to which they belong. Germans are

74

from Germany, Chinese from China, Egyptians from Egypt, Mexicans from Mexico, and black Americans from where? Of all the nationalities in America, black Americans are the only ethnic group that is not called by its true national name. This is quite interesting. We see here that the black Americans lack a nationality. Why? The reason is that the Lord God of Heaven and Earth has permitted the enemies of the African Judean to take away our true nationality. Do we have any biblical proof of this? . . . Yes! We do. "They have said, Come, and let us cut them off from being a nation; that the name of Israel will be no more in remembrance" (Psalm 83:4–5).

The conspiracy to cut blacks off from being a nation began in ancient times and continued unto the present day (Exodus 1:8–22). In the cemetery of horror in America, the slavemasters called blacks by many scornful names except those of their true nationalities. Some of these names are blackbird, blacky, tar baby, coon, crow (black like a crow) negra, colored, pic-kaninny, Negro, and nigger. Some of these names have passed from usage; however, a few of them still linger in our current society. When I was a little boy living in central New Jersey, I was called "Nigger" and "darky" many times. At that time, I would see whites tanning in the sun; this contradiction confused me, and it was not until years later that I realized that whites really did not like white skin.

It was understood by many people that black Americans had been imported from Africa, but the term "African" was never used as an honorable word, nor was it used frequently the terms widely used were "Negro" and "colored." Why did they use the word *African* infrequently? Although the name Africa is not the name of a nationality but a continent with many nations and tribes, the white-supremacists made sure that they did not call blacks Africans. Their objective was clear; they did not want blacks to identify with Africa at all, because Africa was the seat of the earliest civilizations and Africa is where the original black Hebrew Israelites developed

(Egypt and Ethiopia). From the mother, a person receives his nourishment and guidance. Mother Africa is like a mighty tree; the black man in America was cut off from the roots of this tree. As a result, the black man died socially. Blacks are suffering under the curse of God for disobedience. "Thou shall become an astonishment, a proverb and a byword among all nations wither the lord shall lead thee [in captivity]"—Indeed, for many years the black man in South, Central, and North America, who is the true Israelite, has become an astonishment to all races. An *astonishment* means a sad, pitiful amazement. The general attitude of some black people is so disgraceful that it motivates other races to observe us with astonishment. Just to give you one case out of thousands, I witnessed a Korean selling his fruits and vegetables from a vending stand at Thirteenth and Market streets in Philadelphia. Suddenly, the Korean saw and heard three black men standing on the opposite corner using loud foul language and acting like d—— fools. The Korean shook his head in disbelief and astonishment. Now, I shall explain the meaning of the words *proverb* and *byword*.

The words *proverb* and *byword* actually have the same meaning here in the thirty-seventh verse. The Webster's New Collegiate Dictionary says that a proverb is "a name, person, or thing that has become a byword." Let us take careful notes of how this same dictionary defines the word *byword*: "a nickname; a person or thing taken proverbially as a type; usually in a bad sense; hence, an object of scorn." Now, we understand that the words *proverb* and *byword* are nicknames used in a scornful manner in substitution for our true nationality. As I have mentioned previously, the words *Negro, nigger*, and so on are nicknames used in substitution for blacks' true nationality, which is Hebrew Israelites.

The early Europeans who came to America assigned these scornful bywords to blacks and they continue to live and grow in our minds like wild weeds. These names have been planted

76

so deeply into the psyches that they call each other by the word *nigger* more often than whites do black people. You have heard the expressions "that nigger stole my money" or "a nigger ain's s——t." The early whites gave blacks these nicknames so that they would not remember their true nationality. Now, blacks know that they are still under the deadly curse as spoken by the prophet Moses. How do I know this? Because black people have not cast aside many of our slavemasters' ways and ideas. In the next paragraph, I shall show how the word *Negro* was set on fire (discarded) and in its place, blacks made the word *black* fashionable.

The term "black" developed out of the civil-rights struggle of the 1960s when Stokely Carmichael, the grand leader of the Student Nonviolent Coordinating Committee, harangued us on "black power." At that time, black Americans acquired a new awareness of black pride; blacks threw the hair processes out of the window and the Afro style became the new look. The widespread usage of the word *black* instead of the antiquated words *Negro* and *colored* was a step forward. Nevertheless, we have not arrived yet at a uniform word to designate the nationality of the black people in America. However, I have told you that blacks are the original Israelites.

Most Americans use the word *black* in the wrong context. The word *black* is an adjective, and it should only be used to describe a noun or pronoun—for example, a black man or a black shoe. There is one instance when the word *black* is used incorrectly. It is as follows: There are various ethnic groups in America: the Germans, the French, the Irish, the Spanish, the Koreans, and the blacks. Do you observe anything inconsistent in the above statement? Your answer ought to be an absolute yes! The word *blacks* should be substituted with the words *Afro-Americans* or *Afro-Israelites*. Now, if we want to describe variations in color, we can rewrite the statement like this: There are various colors in the American population such as brown, yellow, white, and black. If we continue to use the

first statement, which gives a nationality to other races such as German, and at the same time we use the word *black* what we are doing is depriving black of a nationality. In short, the word *black* should be discarded if it is the intention of the speaker or writer to refer to a nationality, and it can be retained if he wishes to refer to a description of color.

Retaining any signs of the slave mentality is equal to holding on to the curses. The Creator God placed blacks under the curse of the bywords so that their nationality would be taken away; as a consequence of this deprivation or taking away of nationality, most Afro-Americans don't identify with Afro-Israelite culture.

The Creator God said that he would scatter Afro-Israelites into corners (this means from one end of the earth to the other end) and would make the remembrance of them cease from among men (Deuteronomy 32:26). After the slave traders took the Israelites from the African coast (see *Babylon to Timbuktu*), they deported them to South, Central, and North America— even to most islands of the Caribbean Sea. Don't you know that the black people in the western hemisphere are not supposed to know that they are the true Israelites and when they hear this news it is supposed to sound incredible to them, for the Creator said he would make the remembrance of them cease among men. For century after century, the black man in America thought that his true nationality was Negro, and some old-timers still hold on to this scornful byword today. Nevertheless, the spirit of the Creator is moving among the black people, and many have rejected this infamous word, *Negro,* and have returned to their true African-Israelite ancestry. This is the destiny of the black man in America, and the ultimate objective is the repossession of the land of Israel after the Battle of Armageddon.

Again, the Creator was tempted to say in Deuteronomy 32:26–28 that he would destroy the remembrance of the Afro-

American Israelites completely: "Were it not that I feared the wrath of the enemy, lest their adversaries should behave themselves strangely and lest they should say, our hand is high [meaning they are powerful and the white man puts the curse on the Israelites] and the lord has not done all of this." Indeed, the Creator put the curses on Afro-Israelites (Deuteronomy 28:15). He gave man the power to perform this. In the "latter day," "the lord shall judge this people [Israelites] and repent himself for his servants [Israelites] when he seeth their power is gone" (Deuteronomy 32:36). The black man in America is the only race that does not have any power, and does not use what little power he has properly.

Remember that the loss of nationality is a curse, but the darkness and blindness that has fallen on the Israelites (black Americans) is only for a "measure" of time, a limited time, and in the "latter days" (which is now) shall enlightenment and deliverance come to the Israelites (Leviticus 26:44, 45; Jeremiah 30:1–11; Romans 11:25–26; and Daniel 12: 1-4) but before enlightenment arrives, the Creator said the Israelites would serve other gods: "And the Lord shall scatter thee among all people from one end of the earth even until the other; and there thou shall serve *other gods* [italics the author's] which neither thou nor thy fathers have known, even wood and stone" (Deuteronomy 28:64).

The point I want to emphasize in this verse is the "serving of other gods." What does the Creator of the heavens and earth mean when he says "thou shall serve other gods?" He means more than just bowing down to idols made of wood and stone. You must understand that each religion throughout the world has its own dogma, traditions, rules, ideology, philosophy, and history, and when you conform and obey their rules, you are serving other gods. The Creator commanded us not to copy the ways of other nations ("Learn not the ways of the heathens for the way of the heathens are in

vain"– Jeremiah 10:1). From the days that the Creator brought the Afro-Israelites out of Egypt (in Africa) until the present day, they have been learning and adopting the culture of their enemies and oppressors, and the more they try to be like their persecutors, the more they detest us. As a social historian and interpreter of history, I conclude that the most destructive force that undermined and precluded the development of the black community was the extremism of the blacks, desire to be like white people and to get along with them, rather than to get along with their fellow blacks. As a result, black people forgot how to get along with each other. The time the African Israelites arrived in the western hemisphere was the time that the indotrination and learning of the ways of the other nationalities began, with systematic regimentation.

The Afro-Israelites, during slavery, served the slavemasters physically and mentally; they learned the psychology and values of white supremacy, which were pernicious to their own welfare. They learned and believed that whiteness was superior and blackness was inferior. Even some still say, "If you are white, you are right; if you are black, get back; if you are brown, stick around; if you are yellow, you are a better fellow."

The proponents of white supremacy in America endeavored to justify slavery by saying that the blacks were uncivilized and not Christians; they used this same rationale to justify white supremacy. The black people are descendants of a great black civilization that existed for thousands of years. The whites "uncivilized" them and made them savages after bringing them to America; this purely meant that the political, educational, and religious system in the United States brainwashed the black man and stripped him of everything that was refined or virtuous. Gradually, they took away the blacks' history, language, and culture and prohibited them from learning to read and write. They took the little children away from

their mothers and fathers and sold them to other masters; they taught these children about white gods, angels, and heroes, not black heroes. They taught that everything white was right, pure, great, and good and everything black was ugly, dirty, inferior, incapable, wrong, and evil. The religious philosophy of white supremacy dehumanized the Afro-Hebrews; white supremacists did not recognize blacks as human beings, but placed them on the same level as animals. This is the reason they branded their slaves with hot irons, just like they branded their cattle. Supreme Court Chief Justice Taney ruled, in the Dred Scott case, that no "Negro had any rights that a white man must respect." A slave could not take his master to court for any mistreatment. All avenues for justice and help were closed to him; he was utterly helpless and felt inferior.

In the process of time, the black man began to believe in the superiority of the white man's system. He bowed to the white man, served him in every aspect of his life, and worshipped him as god. Moreover, the masters painted a white Jesus and gave it to the black man to serve as god. As a result, it was easy for the black man to obey and believe the white man without question. In truth, whether some of us want to admit it or not, the white man became the black man's god. They employed white standards and values to decide what was right or wrong. In addition, many put very little credence in what other black men said. Most blacks serve the educational religious system in America. It is an oppressive system that thrives and supports itself on the exploitation of the blacks and the poor. For this reason, the existing system cannot render full justice or share the wealth of this country. When we hear the verdicts handed down by many of the courts in this country, we know the kind of justice black men receive. "Know the truth and the truth shall set you free," and where do you find the truth? Not on your eyelids, not at the tip of

your nose, but at the bottom of the well. Stop serving the god of white supremacy and cast away the curse.

Psychological Curses

Psychological curses are those that exert a mental strain on the mind; these curses muster fear, depression, worry, agony, lost of self-esteem, and hopelessness. Some of these curses are explained below.

And thou shall grope at noonday, as the blind gropeth in darkness, and thou shall not prosper in thy ways: and thou shall be only oppressed and spoiled evermore and no man shall save thee."
                                            Deuteronomy 28:59

The word *grope* means to cautiously feel and find one's way. Many people ask the question "What does 'as the blind gropeth in darkness' mean, when, in fact, a blind man cannot see anyway?" One African Israelite answered this question thus: "All my life, I have read this verse, and I did not understand it until the other night when I saw a blind man walking. In the daytime, there are people around to guide him." This verse is a very profound verse when you reflect on its deep meaning. It refers to the severe suffering and agony that the Afro-Israelites would endure in their land of persecution. The suffering of a blind man who is trying to find his way late at night in a strange place and there is no one around to guide him—may God have mercy on his soul!

And thou shall be mad for the sight of thine eyes which thou shall see
                                            Deuteronomy 28:34

Many slaves suffered insanity, madness and hysteria when they saw the slavemasters beat, rape, kill, and sell their loved ones.

"And the Lord shall scatter thee among all people, from one

end of the earth even unto the other—And among these nations shall thou find no ease, neither shall the sole of thy foot rest: but the Lord shall give thee a trembling heart, and failing of eyes and sorrow of mind.

Deuteronomy 28:64-65

Slavery was so harsh and cruel in America that many slaves committed suicide and infanticide. As I explain these verses to you, I am positive you can understand that these curses are applicable, 100 percent, to the black man in the Americas, more so than anyone else in the world.

And thy life shall hang in doubt before thee; and thou shall fear day and night and shall have none assurance of thy life.

Deuteronomy 28:66

For centuries, the destiny and lives of Afro-Americans remained in the hand of white people. Although President Lincoln promulgated the emancipation of the slaves in 1863 and the federal government promised protection for the freemen, the Ku Klux Klan emerged to terrorize, intimidate, and kill the Afro-Israelites ("thy life shall hand in doubt before thee"). Eric Lincoln, in his book *The Negro Pilgrimage in America*, states that between 1900–1931 there were 1, 886 lynchings in America, and this figure does not include the murder of blacks by arson, poison, clubbing, strangulation, or gunfire. [3] moreover, there has been reported a rash of murders of black males, men and youths, throughout America, most of them unsolved and racially related during the last two years. Many of these murders occurred in Buffalo, New York, and other cities. This information was reported by ABC News reporter Ted Koppel on "Nightline."

And thou shall fear day and night and shall have none assurance of thy life.

The prophetical curses were proclaimed by Moses and they shall continually plague us until we return to our God. Blacks had better wake up before it is to late. The Ku Klux Klan and other right wing organizations are on the upsurge. Black people must plan, organize, sacrifice, instruct, and control their economy and community. This is the first step.

> In the morning thou shall say, would God it were even! and at even thou shall say, would God it were morning! for the fear of thine heart where with thou shall fear, and for the sight of thine eyes which thou shall see.
>
> Deuteronomy 28:67

Fear, death, and destruction remained with the black from the moment the slavers took him aboard the slave ships until the present day. Throughout the summer and fall of 1919, more than twenty race riots erupted in the United States, like swarms of locusts, and blood flowed like water in the streets of the American cities.

The worse race riot engulfed the city of Chicago, where whites killed a lonely black boy because he chose to go to a white beach. The boy just wanted to show the whites how much he loved them, and it cost him his life and the lives of many more blacks. The riot ensued for thirteen days, left 38 people dead and 537 injured, and about one thousand black families were made homeless before the National Guard restored order.

Horrible episodes like these caused thousands of black people to feel deep sorrow and hopelessness in the American dream that invariably resulted in a nightmare. It is terrible enough for an individual to feel a condition of despair, but when an entire race becomes a victim to it, the whole social structure collapses. This is precisely what happened to the black man in America, and this hopelessness continues even until today, because we are still suffering under the curses of

God. We deliberately refuse to obey his laws. As a result, we are punished. The Creator God said, "And I will set my face against you, and ye shall be slain before your enemies, they that hate you shall reign over you" (Leviticus 26:17).

The above verse is crystal clear. For centuries, the black man in America has been willfully murdered and those that hated blacks have ruled over them. The Ku Klux Klan murdered black people, like they hunted wild geese. Moreover, some police kill black people as if they are on a hunting safari. In the black ghettos throughout America, the police are practically all white and they behave like an occupying army, shooting first and asking a dying man questions later. In the city of Philadelphia alone, and in recent years the police handcuffed victims behind their backs and shot them. I heard when blacks are killed by police, the excuses are usually weak ones like: "My service revolver accidentally went off."

A policeman shooting an unarmed, black man. Read what Moses wrote in Leviticus 26:14, 15, and 17.

These officers were set scot free by juries who were, on the most part, white. During the Cornel Warren case (the dead black victim), Mrs. Warren, the mother of the dead boy, cried pitiful sobs, as she went out of the courtroom with tears running down her face. She repeated over and over, "How could they let him go? How could they let him go? There is no justice! There is no justice!" Many of us can empathize with Mrs. Warren. She was so brokenhearted, faint, and weak as she departed from the court that her lawyer and relative had to support her as she walked down the hall. Mrs. Warren's mental anguish reminds us what God said in Leviticus 26:14, 33, and 36. "But if you will not harken unto me and will not do all these commandments, I will scatter you among the heathen [non-Jews, other nationalities]. And upon them that are left of you, I will send a faintness into their hearts in the lands of their enemies."

Did Mrs. Warren really expect justice? While we are under the curse, we shall not obtain justice until we get the knowledge and power. I shall explain more about power very shortly. To get these officers free, the system did a lot of "wheeling and dealing" and they may passed a lot of money. The sinful world stands on three things: money, money, and more money; the American people worship the "golden calf." In view of this, God will intervene soon to put an end to the injustice.

> Moreover all these curses shall come upon thee, and shall pursue thee, and overtake thee till thou be destroyed; [why?] because thou hearkenedst not unto the voice of the Lord thy God, to keep his commandments and his statutes which he commanded thee
>
> Deuteronomy 22:45

Just as the legal courts punish a man when he violates the laws, likewise the creator God punishes humanity when

we violate his laws. Many have been expelled from their home-land, Israel, for almost 2,000 years, and they are still violating God's laws in our land of captivity the United States. The crimes in the black community are reported to be the highest in the nation; it is so terrible that we cannot even tolerate to live around each other.

> And they [the curses] shall be upon thee for a sign and a wonder and upon thy seed [children] forever.
>
> Deuteronomy 28:46

The Creator, who controls the course of human events in the world, said that these curses will be on the Afro-Israelites and on their seed for a sign. A sign of what? A sign that indicates the fact that the people who suffered the curses are those who violated God's laws, as stipulated in the Bible; also, it is a sign that the sufferers of the curses are the descendents of the twelve tribes of Israel, whether the sufferers know it or not. These curses will be on blacks forever until they cease from evil ways. Then the curses will be removed from them (Deuteronomy 30:1–13).

It is written that when all of these blessing and curses have come upon blacks and if they shall remember these curses (sorrows) among the nations where the Lord has scattered them and shall return unto the Lord and obey his laws, then the Lord will remove the curses and return them to their homeland, Israel. Then he will bless them above their great ancestors, and they shall be the head and not the tail, and he will put these curses upon their enemies (Deuteronomy 30:1–7, 28:13).

The Miami Race Riot

The riot in Miami, Florida, in 1980 was the worst racial disturbance in over a decade in the land of "liberty and justice for all." The death toll reached fifteen. Blacks and whites were beaten and, in a few cases, mutilated. The property damage exceeded more than a hundred million dollars. And what initiated it all? When we scrutinize the white-supremacy kangaroo-court system in the "land of the free and the home of the brave," we recognize that the court system failed miserably to punish those guilty of murder.

The Miami riots began on May 17, 1980, because an all-white jury exonerated four white police officers of blame in beating a black insurance agent, Arthur McDuffie, to death. The facts of the McDuffie case are really outrageous. Although the stories differ on which officer may have struck the first blow, there is a consensus that several policemen bestially beat McDuffie and later falsified the police reports to give the impression that it was an accident.

On December 17, 1979, as revealed by police reports, McDuffie drove his motorcycle through a red light, and when the police pursued him, he tried to outrun them. The stories vary as to whether McDuffie crashed or gave himself up. The first police report said he crashed and struck his head on the sidewalk. Moreover, it said he then resisted the police with such great strength that they had to forcibly subdue him. This becomes an unbelievable story when one considers the kind of injury anyone receives in a motorcycle accident. After McDuffie was halted, several policemen with nightsticks sat on him. He was on the ground, motionless, and one of them beat him about the head.

This kind of beating inflicted horrible injury. The coroner said McDuffie's skull had been "cracked like an egg." A Dade County medical examiner said it was "tantamount to falling four stories."

Before Moses died, he predicted that if we would not keep God's law, all these curses would happen to us: "And thy life shall hang in doubt before thee; and thou shall fear day and night and shall have none assurance of thy life" (Deuteronomy 28:66).

In some cases, when a white person kills a black man or woman, the murderer goes free. In certain areas this might have happened right in your community. And so it was in the McDuffie case his murderers got off scot free. How did this happen? The answer is simple; blacks are under the curse of God Almighty and don't have any power. This is what the establishment did in Miami: They removed the trial from Miami to another area of the state. Secondly, they chose an all-white jury and reduced the jury from the traditional twelve members to six: the black man got half of something that was not worth anything in the first place. It was as if you were supposed to get a whole apple and your exploiters handed you one-half of a rotten one. The black man in this country will always be shortchanged, because he is under the curse and does not have any power.

The whites have the power. That is why they can change the rules of the game and get away with it. The black man is not supposed to have any real power, because he disobeyed the Almighty. Listen what the Almighty said through the mouth of his prophet Moses (author's italics):

But if ye will not hearken unto me and will not do all these Commandments . . . I will set my face against you, and ye shall be *slain* before your *enemies*: they that hate you shall reign over you . . . And I will break the pride of your power; and I will make your heaven as iron, and your earth as brass [The Almighty will make our troubles heavy as iron and brass.] . . . And ye shall have no power to stand before your enemies.

Leviticus 26:14, 17, 19, 37

89

Isn't the prediction of the Almighty crystal clear? At this juncture, if you don't understand the substance of what I have written, then, I only can say, it is not for *you* to understand. Now, a little more about injustice.

The injustice that is constantly committed against the black race in the "land of the stars and stripes" is watched by the entire world, and they do not approve of the way "Uncle Sam" treats his black adopted nephews. Because of this stain on the reputation of America, the prestige of the United States has fallen considerably on the global scale.

Let's not deal in rhetoric, but let the facts speak for themselves. Just recently, in the year 1979, the students in Iran stormed the American embassy and captured the personnel. Soon, a directive came down from the high echelon to release the black hostages. The Iranians did not hesitate to disclose the reasons for their release; they said that the black man suffered enough in the land of America and they sympathized with him.

How to Get Unity and Power

In order to obtain power, we must begin to respect and obey the laws of the Almighty. I realize by now that some of you probably think that I sound like a person who plays the same old tune over and over again, but there is no other way of getting around it! We have tried other ways, and they have utterly failed, so let's try the way of the Almighty.

First of all, in order to acquire power, it is essential to possess unity, and in order to obtain unity, it is imperative to remove the curses that preclude or prevent the acquisition of unity. It is the flagrant violation of God's law that retains the curse on us and prevents unity, and that law is as follows: "Thou shall love thy neighbor as thyself." "Thy neighbor" means thy brother (Leviticus 19:17), who belongs to the same race as you belong. Also, the Almighty instructed us to love

the stranger (a member of another race) (Leviticus 19:33–34. However, we are instructed to love our own race first. ("Charity begins at home.") "Love thy neighbor as thyself"—in essence, this means after you have loved and done for thyself, then love and do for thy neighbor. In view of this, many black people have the whole thing backward. They love first other races instead of themselves; they will, many times, recognize and greet other races before their own kind; they will believe and trust another race before they trust their own. The way black people behave is like "putting the cart before the horse" as if they expected the cart to lead the horse. This is the reason that blacks have not attained good result (power, unity and so forth) during captivity in America; their minds are in captivity.

With this kind of attitude prevailing among blacks, can you say that they love each other? No! Since they don't love each other and can't stand to be around each other, then, I ask you, with these negative attitudes, how can they come together in unity? They can't! Because they have violated one of the main laws of God: "Thou shall love thy neighbor as thyself." As a result of this violation, the curse and punishment remains with blacks and they are just as divided now as freemen as they were divided under slavery.

Here is a list of some of the laws of the Almighty Creator, which we violate, that are essential for the maintenance of an orderly society or community or acquisition of unity.

1. "Thou shalt not kill" (Exodus 20:13).
2. "Thou shalt not steal" (Exodus 20:15).
3. "Thou shalt not commit adultery" (Exodux 20:14).
4. "Thou shalt not bear false witness [perjury]" (Exodus 20:16).
5. "Thou shalt not covet [want] thy neighbor's goods" (Exodus 20:17).
6. "Honor thy father and thy mother" (Exodus 20:12).

7. "Thou shalt have no other gods before me" (Exodus 20:3).
8. "And he that smiteth [beat] his father or his mother shall surely be put to death" (Exodus 21:15).
9. "And he that curseth his father or his mother shall be put to death" (Exodus 21:17).
10. "Thou shalt neither vex a stranger, nor oppress him: for ye [children of the Israelites] were strangers in the land of Egypt [Africa]" (Exodus 22:21).
11. "Ye shalt not afflict any widow or fatherless child" (Exodus 22:22).
12. "If thou lend money to any of my people that is poor by thee, thou shall not be to him as an usurer, neither shall thou lay usury [interest]" (Exodus 22:25).
13. "Ye shalt not therefore oppress one another [exploit or get over on]" (Leviticus 25:17).
14. "Ye shalt not steal, neither deal falsely, neither lie one to another" (Leviticus 19:11).
15. "Thou shalt not defraud thy neighbor, neither rob him" (Leviticus 19:13).
16. "Thou shalt not go up and down as a tale bearer among thy people" (Leviticus 19:16).
17. "If a man also lie with mankind, as he lieth with a woman, both of them have committed an abomination" (Leviticus 20:13).
18. "And if a man lie with a beast, he shall surely be put to death and ye shall slay the beast."
19. "And if a woman approach unto any beast, and lie down there to, thou shall kill the woman and the beast" (Leviticus 20:16).
20. "Thou shalt not avenge, nor bear any grudge against the children of thy people, but thou shalt love thy neighbors as thyself" (Leviticus 19:18).

21. "Do not prostitute thy daughter to cause her to be a whore" (Leviticus 19:29).
22. "Ye shall do no unrighteous in judgement, in meteyard, in weight or in measure [scales]" (Leviticus 19:35).
23. "Just balance, just weight . . . shall ye have" (Leviticus 19:36).
24. "Thou shalt not hate thy brother in thy heart; thou shalt in any wise rebuke thy neighbor [tell him about it, if he does anything wrong] and not suffer sin upon him" (Leviticus 19:17).

There are two ways to hate thy brother: (1) When you believe that he did something wrong or behaved in a way you detest or (2) because you hate yourself. In other words, you hate him and yourself because the skin is black and you have the notion that black people are racially inferior; this kind of hatred is referred to as self-hatred. Self-hatred results by lacking the knowledge of the greatness of your ancestors and the contribution that they rendered for the advancement of world civilization and the betterment of mankind. You can read about the great exploits of black people by reading my first book *From Babylon to Timbuktu*.

Some of us don't know our great history, because our oppressors deprived us of it; they distorted our history, deliberately and systematically misinterpreted our history and flavored it with race prejudice in order to leave us with an inferiority complex. One story out of many that I heard when I was a boy was that the Africans swung through the trees like monkeys, but in reality, the only people whom I ever saw swinging through trees were Tarzan and Jane, yelling like mad people. As we can see, this kind of self-hatred is derived from not having racial pride and a knowledge of our history.

The Almighty Creator directed us to love our brothers

93

and sisters; now, it is logical to conclude that he wants us to love ourselves, because he said, "Love thy neighbor as thyself." Indirectly, he is saying, "Love thyself, and anyone who does not love himself violates God's laws." He wants us to be happy with ourselves but not to be egotistical. If an individual doesn't love himself or his race, how in the world can he work together for his community or humanity? It is not likely. This is the basic reason: The black race in America finds it an insurmountable problem to muster concerted effort to accomplish our objective; as a consequence, we are impotent and incapable in acquiring real social, economic, and political power.

For example, if we would have had unity, organization, and power, the black people in Miami would not have had to succumb to the final resort of rampant violence to release and demonstrate their rage against repetitive injustice. On the other hand, if blacks had strong power and magnanimous and dedicated leaders, they would have been mandated by the black people to make sure that the trial was not moved to another area of the state; they would have made sure that at least half of the jurors were black, and they would have made sure that the jury was not reduced from twelve to six members.

Summary

Some of you might ask the question "Couldn't some of these curses apply to other races?" Yes, some of them could, but not even one half of the curses apply to others. However, in order for the prophecy of Moses to be confirmed, all of them must apply to the same people intended. When all of these curses apply, then it shall be confirmed who are the original Israelites. Considering the evidence demonstrated in *From Babylon to Timbuktu* and the evidence supplied in this book, I must conclude, without any doubt, that all these curses are applicable to the black man in the western hemisphere;

make no mistake about it! Earlier, I mentioned five or six classifications of curses:

1. Worldwide dispersal
2. Psychological Curses
3. Biological or physical curses
4. Economic curses
5. Loss of identity or nationality

These curses do not apply to the white races, because they simply do not fit the total description of these curses. The Europeans were not imported to America in large numbers by compulsion as captive slaves; only a few were indentured servants for a limited number of years. But the vast majority of the Europeans came to America as free immigrants. The Europeans did not sustain the destruction of their manhood, history, identity, language, or culture, nor did they lose the protection of the law. The Europeans were not exploited economically but became the masters of exploitation; the Europeans did not sustain chronic psychological degradation or gross physical mutilation comparable to that of the black man. On the contrary, he inflicted the psychological and physical punishment. In closing, let me add that, according to history and the Bible, all of these curses were supposed to happen to a black people, because the original Israelites were black with wooly hair. (For additional information on the blackness of the ancient Israelites read Jeremiah 14:2; Jeremiah 8:21; Revelations 1:14–15; Ezekiel 40:3; Daniel 7:9; Songs of Solomon 1:5, and Lamentations 5:10.)

Notes

1. Daniel Mannix, *Black Cargo* (New York: Viking Press, 1962).
2. E. Lincoln, *The Negro Pilgrimage in America* (New York: Bantam Books, 1961), 72.
3. Lincoln, *Negro Pilgrimage*, 81.

4

The Resurrection of a Dead Nation

Some people have believed for many years the "dry bones" (in the thirty-seventh chapter of Ezekiel) refers to the resurrection of billions of dead people at the time of the coming of the Messiah. They couldn't be further from the truth. When we study the complete Bible, and all the book of Ezekiel, we see that there is clear proof that the "dry bones" refer only to an ancient race and their sons, and they do not refer to the actual dead found in graves. In this chapter, you will find a logical meaning of the "dry bones" and historical and current facts to reveal the true meaning of God.

God brought Ezekiel (in a vision) to a deep valley that was full of bones. Then God said to him, "Can these bones live?"

Ezekiel replied, "Thou knowest."

Then God said to Ezekiel, "Prophesy to these bones and speak unto them, 'O ye dry bones, hear the word of the Lord.' And I will lay sinews upon you, and will bring up flesh upon you and cover you with skin, and put breath in you, and ye shall live. And ye shall know that I am the Lord." So Ezekiel prophesied as he was commanded, and as he prophesied, there was a noise and a shaking, and the bones came together, bone to his bone (Ezekiel 37:4–7).

The process of the bones coming together formed skeletons. What does this mean? The joining of the bones symbolize the uniting and the building of families. During the period of slavery, there was virtually no concept of family or formal legal marriage. Children were taken away from their mothers; fathers, brothers, and sisters were sold to remote plantations. With the advent of freedom after the Civil War, the liberated slaves began to search for lost relatives. Lerone Bennett, Jr., tells this touching story: "In the first sweet flush of freedom men and women trudged dusty roads asking sad questions. 'Has anyone here seen Sarah?' 'Do you know a man named Sam?' Many stories from this era tell of men who married only to discover later that they had married a cousin or a sister." [1] Nonetheless, the bones of the families were coming together.

> And when I beheld, lo, the sinews and the flesh came up upon them and the skin covered them above: but there was no breath in them.
>
> Ezekiel 37:8

Sinews are tendons; they connect the muscle to the bones. Also, sinews and flesh represent the coming together of the families. The skin symbolizes the acquisition of education, college degrees, good professional jobs, new homes and cars— in other words, anything that contributes to a person's outer appearance or prestige, just as the skin adds to the physical appearance and beauty of the human body. In spite of the fact that a number of black people have high-paying jobs, the vast majority of black people are living in abject poverty, ignorance, confusion, in crime-infested areas, devoid of the proper leadership. Something is wrong, something is lacking in the black man's community; our educated people, with all their Ph.D.'s, have not been able to solve the problem. All the civil-rights bills and the Supreme Court decision have not

97

solved our problems; integration has not proven itself as a solution for our manifold problems. Since the assassination of Malcolm and King, black people have gone down, down, down, down, down, and down. Now we have reached "rock bottom," with President Reagan putting the knife to most affirmative-action programs.

Black people are in an extreme state of disillusionment and confusion. It reminds me of the Temptations' record "Ball of Confusion." Black men and women were walking or standing on the street corner looking like zombies, not knowing where to go, not knowing what to do, but only thinking to do in one another. (The more exact expression is "to get over on one another.") When Kunta Kinte (in *Roots*) first arrived in America, he saw the other slaves; he said they all looked like zombies. He meant that they behaved as if they had been drugged; the old slaves did not have their original states of mind. Kunta Kinte could detect the difference, because he was a new young arrival. Today, the black man acts like a zombie, under a deep sleep. Many of us are the "living dead" without hope, without purpose, without guidance, and without a destiny!

The prophet Ezekiel saw these "living dead." The bones, sinews, flesh, and skin came together; nevertheless, they were likened to corpses in the valley. The valley is America. All of these bodies that Ezekiel saw had no life, and the black man in America has no life; those ingredients necessary to sustain a viable, living black community are grossly lacking. (There will be more about these ingredients a little later.)

> Then he said unto me prophesize unto the wind, prophesize son of man, and say to the wind [breath], thus say the Lord God; come from the four winds [the four directions], oh, breathe and breathe upon these slain that they may live.
>
> Ezekiel 37:9

Although many black people have acquired advancement

into the mainstream of the American society, nevertheless, in the eyesight of God, He has considered us a slain (dead) people, because the masses of the black people are still on the bottom of the political, economic, and social level and are not guided in the proper direction.

1. Black people are dead, because the black leaders are divided and some leaders are not responsive to the adequate needs of the people.
2. Black people are dead, because the police can sometimes murder a black man handcuffed behind his back and the police will be set free.
3. Black people are dead, because they have to depend on those that hate them for a livelihood.
4. Black people are dead, because they do not own or control the businesses in their own neighborhoods, but new aliens often control the businesses.
5. Black people are dead, because their houses and buildings are vandalized, boarded up, and disfigured with grafitti.
6. Black people are dead, because they don't help each other.
7. Black people are dead, because the behavior of students is terrible and the educational level is in a sorrowful state.
8. Black people are dead, because disunity, mistrust, and -disrespect exist between black males and females.
9. Black people are dead, because the unemployment rate is the highest in the nation and a qualified black female can get a job quicker than a qualified black male (in affirmative-action programs, because a black woman is less of a threat to the white male than a black male is).
10. Black people are dead, because many of them are

preoccupied with sports, dancing, and music, carrying loud radios in the streets as big as luggage bags. These radios are so loud that the Martians could hear them from their remote red planet.

11. Black people are dead, because so many of them lie to each other perpetually, well knowing that they have no intentions of fulfilling their promises in the first place.

12. Black people are socially dead, because most will not accept the word of another black man unless that word is confirmed by the white power structure, but a Jim Jones from California was able to take 900 black people to their death, all in the name of religion and integration.

13. Black people are dead, because the crime in the black community is the highest in the nation in proportion to the population and most of this crime, which eats like a malignant cancer, destroying the foundation of our community, is committed by blacks against blacks.

Absolutely, blacks are socially and mentally dead for all of the aforementioned reasons.

Considering the fact of the individual advancement of some blacks and the deplorable conditions that prevail in the black community today, this is a contradiction. Every day, we hear and read about the ways other ethnic groups built their social institutions around their cultural heritage. But something is wrong when black social institutions have not arrived at the conclusion that African cultural heritage is a necessary element for the development of a healthy, breathing black community.

So I prophesied as he commanded me and the breath came

into them and they lived and stood up on their feet, an exceedingly great army.

Ezekiel 37:10

What does the breath symbolize? We have learned that the bones, sinews, and flesh represent the unification of dispersed families after the emancipation from slavery and the skin represents the attaining of higher positions in all areas of American life, with the assistance of the federal laws. Nevertheless, this did not solve the gross chronic social problems as experienced and suffered by the masses of the black people. Why? Because the most important element was lacking: the breath. Without this breath of life, the black man in America can be compared to a corpse lying in a $50,000 casket, dressed up in a $500 tuxedo, wearing a $100,000 diamond ring on his finger, a solid gold watch on his wrist, and a pair of $200 shoes on his stinky feet.

The appearance of this black man lying in his luxurious casket dazzles the imagination of many other ethnic groups. They ask the question "What good is his wealth?" He does not have any life, but a deceptive glowing image among the galaxy of peoples of the earth. The other ethnic groups say that the blacks have some movie and television stars, educators, supervisors, doctors, lawyers, engineers, sportsmen, singers and so on. But these blacks that have made it do not help blacks who need help. They let the masses of the blacks linger in the cesspool of ignorance, unemployment, filth, and crime. The few black men and women that have and the masses that don't have, represent the cancerous corpse lying in the casket without breath.

Now, the breath, which is so necessary for the resuscitation of the black man from his state of death and social decay, represents many things, such as: the law and spirit of God, a return to the African-Hebrew-Israelite-Judean identity, nationality, culture, history, and language. It is the acquisition

of tremendous racial pride; it is the removal of the decadent slave mentality. It is black nationalism, is the utilization of this African-Hebrew-Israelite culture to acquire stupendous economical power to help solve the increasing unemployment problem. This breath will revitalize the black man, bring him to life, and impart to him knowledge and the understanding to direct his affairs in every compartment of life so that the masses of black communities will be safe from destroying themselves. Moreover, every other nationality is using the black man in his own home and community. This means that they are exploiting the black man, and the black man allows it.

The sociologists and psychologists for decades offered a multitude of various remedies to lessen the social problems in the black community; those that are responsible for destroying black people will not save black people, nor will the solutions work (which the blacks learned from the oppressor). At the time I write this, we have reached the year 1981; 116 years have passed since the blacks' liberation from physical slavery, and they still don't receive justice in the courts. Furthermore, many Oriental persons can immigrate to this country and overnight they become the blacks' masters. Blacks have been here so long, and it seems that they just can't get themselves together to accomplish anything for the masses. Every conceivable method has been tried but one, and that is the solution of the Creator God. The emergency of the state of affairs in the black community and in the world requires corrective and effective solutions. The solutions that I render in this book are not predicated on European or Western racist views; however, they are founded on Afro-Asian-Hebrew-Israelite interpretations.

After the black man in America acquires his Afro-Israelite culture, the things he needs most are the laws of God and the spirit and will to do these laws. I am convinced that many of you don't want to hear this, but the laws of the Creator are

the only things that will save the black man and even the whole world from complete destruction. Now, the breath that the prophet Ezekiel talked about is nothing but the spirit of God. Listen what the Universal Creative Force said to the Israelites (black people in America): "A new heart also will I give you and a new spirit will I put within you and I will take away the stony heart out of your flesh and I will give you a heart of flesh and I will put my spirit within you and cause you to walk in my statutes and you shall keep my ordinances and do them" (Ezekiel 36:26).

The expression "stony heart" simply means a hardhearted person who will not do God's laws. The expression that we use today is "coldhearted" or "coldblooded." In the Bible, the prophets refer to Israelites, our black ancestors, as a stiff-necked and rebellious people, a people with stony hearts who would not show mercy to a senior citizen or anyone else but would knock them down in the streets and take their money. On the other hand, the Creator God said he would give his people a "heart of flesh," a "new heart," and a "new spirit." The breath of life that enters the dried bones or the dead black people in America is the new spirit or good spirit as opposed to the evil spirit.

Then he said unto me, son of man, these bones are the whole house of Israel: behold they say that are bones are dried, and our hope is lost; we are cut off for our parts.

Ezekiel 37:11

As you can see, the Creator God revealed to the prophet, in the eleventh verse, who these bones represent. These symbolize the entire house of Israel, which developed from the twelve sons of Jacob and became the twelve tribes of Israel (Genesis 35:23). But at first, the prophet did not know who these bones represented although he was an Israelite. There

103

is profound meaning in the fact that Ezekiel did not recognize the identity of these bones. Can the reader guess?

Some people speculate that these bones represent the resurrection of the dead from their graves. When one has knowledge and understands the interpretation, symbolism of the Scriptures, and God's plan on earth, we are convinced that those who maintain this school of thought are remote from the truth. The prophet Ezekiel did not see dead bodies or skeletons in a burial grave of a cemetery, as we know them. He saw various bones disconnected and scattered over the surface of the valley. The prophets spoke in symbolic language many times, and in due time I shall prove that the dry bones represent the revival and restoration of the people and nation of the Israelites. The symbolism in this chapter, in particular, is extremely profound, and it could not be completely understood until now, the time of the end, which is in our days. Daniel, the holy man of God, said, "And I heard, but I understood not: then said I, O my Lord, what shall be the end of these things [events]? And he said, go thy way, Daniel. [This means "don't ask anymore questions"] for the words are closed up and sealed till the time of the end (Daniel 12:8–9).

Now, that the time of the end has arrived, we can unseal and explain the hidden meaning and symbolism in the Bible, oh my people! First of all, let us remember that the Creator God carried Ezekiel down into a valley that was full of dry bones. Take notice that the bones were not located on the top of a hill but in a valley. This fact indicates the depth or lowness to which the Israelites would be reduced. Generally, men establish cemeteries on high ground, not in valleys.

The prophet walked among these bones and analyzed them in great detail; he saw that they were not even skeletons, but dried, disconnected, unidentifiable bones dispersed over the surface of the valley. The bones had become subjected to all kinds of unimaginative and horrible conditions and became

dried over an exceedingly long period of time. When the Lord asked Ezekiel, "Can these bones [people] live?" he answered, "Thou knowest." Let us analyze the answer of Ezekiel and study its implications. The prophet was actually saying, "I don't think these dried bones can live, but there is nothing impossible with you, O Lord. Thou knowest, not I."

The Lord asked Ezekiel, "Can these bones live?" Black people today paraphrase the same question in their own way: "Do you think that black people will ever get themselves together?"

"Nope! A nigger ain't s———t."

"Do you think that black people will ever do anything right?"

"Nope! I don't know what is wrong with yo' people"

"What do you mean yo' people? They're not my people, but yo' —— people."

Oh, but God knows what is wrong with "yo' people"; they are a dead people.

> Again he said unto me, prophesy unto these bones and say unto them, O ye dry bones, hear the word of the Lord.

The Creator God has issued a proclamation to the Afro-American-Israelites to stop, look, and listen to the word of the Lord. It is the Creator who controls your destiny and the fate of the world, whether you want to realize it or not. I know that many of you don't want to hear anything about religion or God. Your ancestors did not listen to the prophets of old. They would not incline their ears to hear, so I know you are not going to listen to me (Jeremiah 44:1–5). Many of you don't want to change your evil ways or your life-styles. The forces of good must unite to fight the forces of evil, or else the world or our community will not be safe for anybody. The black man and woman in America are commanded by

God to hear the word of the Lord: "O ye dry bones." Will you listen? This is the first step to take in order to save our neighborhood from social decay, or are you too busy or addicted to the sound of music or to the television shows? You are addicted to "Dallas," "Good Times," "Dynasty, "What's Happening," "Love Boat," "The Jeffersons," and, of course, "Fantasy Island." Yes! You are living in a world of fantasy, so don't be surprised one day when you return home to find out you are missing all your furniture. Set your priorities in order and "hear the word of the Lord, O dry bones." The Creator can not help us until we listen. A black man said to me last year, "How can you make the assertion that we are Israelites when we don't possess any records or tradition of being the children of Israel?" My retort to him was like this: If the prophet Ezekiel, who was also a priest and a living Israelite at the time of his vision, could not recognize the identity of the dead, dried bones scattered in the valley, how can you expect the dead bones (black people) to know their own identity? The dead cannot lead the dead. Just as the identity of the bones had to be revealed to the prophet, the Creator God had made known to me and other Israelites the true identity of the black man in America. Again, the fact that Ezekiel did not recognize the dried bones means that most people in the world would not be able to recognize the identity of the black Americans, not even the white Jews; so don't be surprised one bit if a white Jew says that black Americans are not Israelites. For the most part, white Jews are converts to the Jewish religion in the first place.

> Therefore prophesy and say unto them, thus says the Lord God, behold, my people, I will open your graves, and cause you to come up out of your graves, and bring you into the land of Israel.
>
> Ezekiel 37:12

Their ancestry goes back to time of King David

Rabbi Matthews is shown holding the Torah (the five books of Moses). He organized a congregation of Ethiopian Hebrews in 1918 in New York City and ordained many rabbis. Inset shows some Ethiopian Israelites learning more about the Hebrew culture in Israel.

Again, we must remember that the word *graves* here does not mean a big hole dug in the ground, but the meaning is symbolic and refers to the nations that hold the black Americans powerless in slavery, captivity, oppression, and a state of ignorance. How do we know this? "I will open your graves" means that the Creator God will unlock the gross condition of ignorance we are in that binds us to impotence and social decay. He will remove from us the darkness of the Western World and give us the light of the East. ("I will cause you to come up out of your graves and bring you into the land of Israel.") In order for the Creator to bring us into the land Israel, the grave has to be the countries of our slavery, captivity, and oppression.

Is There a White Jewish Bias?

During the 1970s, the General Assembly of the United Nations introduced and approved a number of resolutions condemning Zionism as a form of racism. From 1870 to about 1948, most of the land acquired in Palestine by European Jews was purchased from the Arabs. However, around 1948 and extending into the future, the Israeli government occupied Arab land they took in battle for strategic military reasons; the consequence of the Arabs losing was the Arabs lost these lands, consequently creating a horrible refugee problem. This was the basis for the anti-Jewish resolutions in the United Nations condemning Zionism as a form of racism.

It is not my intention at this time to deal with the Palestinian refugee problem. I will leave that for another book. However, it is my fervent desire to analyze and investigate in order to determine if bias exists within the world Jewish organizations or within the Israeli governmental apparatus and if so to what extent. Let us commence our investigation by looking backward into history.

108

We must remember that Jacob, the father of the twelve tribes of Israel, departed from Canaan (now Israel) and went down to the neighboring African country of Egypt with his family of sixty-nine people. Here, in this African environment, the Israelites multiplied until they numbered over a million people. Yes! Along the Nile River in Mother Africa was the incubator of the ancient Israelite people. It is common knowledge now that Hebrew-Israelites lived in Africa before they existed on any other continent. Finally, the Israelites led by Moses and Joshua established themselves in the African country of Canaan, then controlled by Egypt. Here they constructed a nation ruled by many kings: Saul, David, Solomon and so on. After existing as a nation for over 200 years, the Israelite nation split in two and was on the verge of civil war. The southern kingdom was called Judah, and the northern kingdom retained the name of Israel.

Finally, a new empire arose, Assyria. It conquered the northern kingdom of Israel and dispersed the Israelites in the Middle East in 722 B.C. About 135 years later, another world power, Babylon, conquered the kingdom of Judah and carried the Judeans (Jews) as captive slaves to Babylon. After the Judeans had remained in Babylon (modern Iraq) for seventy years, Babylon was conquered by yet another power: the Persians. King Cyrus of Persia permitted the Judeans to return to the land of Judah and to rebuild Jerusalem and the temple beginning in 516–444 B.C. The land of Israel always stood in the way of new conquering powers: It was Greece in 332 B.C. and then Rome in 68 B.C. The Romans put a complete end to the Judean State in A.D. 70 with a great slaughter and taking them into captivity. The aforementioned world powers conquered the land of Israel from the north. As always, marching armies create a refugee problem; consequently, over a period of seven hundred years, hundreds of thousands of Israelites fled to the bordering African state of Egypt, and by the year 1 A.D. there were more than 1 million Hebrew Israelites in

the three African countries of Libya, Egypt, and Ethiopia combined, with minor penetrations in the Sahara and other parts of West Africa.

At this juncture of history, the highest concentration of Israelites was in Asia and Africa, but with the Roman era, there began a slow movement to Europe. The Romans transported Israelite slaves to the city of Rome; other Israelites migrated to Rome and other cities in Europe. These black Jews built communities and synagogues, owned white servants, converted many of these servants to the Israelite religion, and intermarried with them. After hundreds of years in Europe, the Israelites became lighter and lighter in color; they began to call themselves Jews or Jewish people. They had practically no contact with the Jews of Africa and Asia. they spoke a new language called Yiddish; it is a German dialect written in letters of the Hebrew alphabet and containing elements of Hebrew, Russian, Polish, and other languages. There developed a complete new culture known as Yiddish culture, modeled after European ways of life. When white supremacy developed in Europe during the sixteenth century, Jewish thought and life began to be flavored with it; this is evident in the white biblical pictures they made and their straightening their hair. They used a different pronunciation in Hebrew, and their religious services changed considerably, compared to those of the Afro-Asian Israelites. They adopted European names such as Sakaloff, Pearlstein, Weinstein, Kleinbaum, Weizmann, and Jabotinsky instead of Hebrew names such as Yaakov, Yirmiyahu, Eshmelek, Eshmelek, Shmuel, Ahaz, and so forth. These Jews removed themselves so far from their once African homeland, that, as a result, they began to think like Europeans. in their new white skin. From then on, they were known as Ashkenazi or German Jews. Most of these Ashkenazi Jews are found in Europe, Australia, South Africa (a racist country), Canada, and the United States.

As the twentieth century arrived, the Jewish institutions in the European world perpetuated the concept that the biblical Israelites were white, to the point of forgetting that the Israelites were black.

In the famous movie titled *The Ten Commandments*, Yul Brynner played the role of the African phaorah and Charlton Heston, with his conspicuously Caucasian features, played the part of Moses, the leader of the African Hebrew slaves. If the ancient Hebrew slaves had been white, performing rigorous work day after day, under the intense heat of the African sun, which reaches 120 degrees, under these conditions, they would have died out completely during the first summer of slavery, because of heat strokes.

The Sephardim or Afro-Asian Israelites

The word *Sephardi* means "Spanish"; it refers to the Afro-Israelites who lived in Portugal and Spain when the Moors ruled that country for seven hundred years. However, its meaning has developed to a much broader usage; its broad meaning is now applied to non-European Israelites or the descendents of them, who lived in Moslem countries or in Afro-Asian countries, period. Another name applied to these Israelites is "Oriental," because they are from Eastern countries or countries with an Eastern culture as opposed to Western European culture. The complexion of these Sephardic Israelites ranges from jet black to high yellow. Many of the Israelites from Iran are yellow, from Morocco they are brown and yellow, from Egypt they are yellow and brown, and from West Africa they are black; in other words, the Israelites in Afro-Asian countries look like the people in those countries. The music and dress of the Israelites in the Moslem world is the same as that of the Moslems in those countries. In addition,

111

the Sephardic Israelites speak the purest Hebrew dialect, and this dialect is the official language of the state of Israel. Another fact that separates the Sephardic Israelites from the Ashkenazic Jews is that the Sephardics never became the perpetrators of racism; color was never an issue to them.

Destruction of the Afro-Asian Israelites

By the sixth century, the black Hebrew Israelites had increased in such large numbers that they were found throughout the Middle East. They had at least two kingdoms in southern Arabia, a kingdom in Ethiopia, large settlements across North Africa and the Sahara Desert, a kingdom just southeast of the Senegal River; there was the Hebrew kingdom of Ghana, and there were numerous Hebrew Israelite settlements all along the West African coast as far south as the country of Angola. Some of these Hebrew Israelites converted to Islam. Others amalgamated into indigenous African tribes, and many were transported as slaves to America. (For detailed information, read *From Babylon to Timbuktu*.)

In order to understand the attitude of European and European Jews toward Afro-Hebrew Israelites, we must, therefore, scrutinize past world events. After the fall of the Roman Empire in the year A.D. 476, Europe slept for a thousand years; this period in Europe was called the Dark Ages. Practically no knowledge derived from Europe. During this same period of time, the hearth of the Afro-Asian world pulsated with tremendous commercial and intellectual activity; also, the Muslims and the black Hebrew Israelites contributed greatly to all the sciences. Gradually, Europe began to be stimulated by the intellectual activity of Africa and Asia, and the Renaissance (or rebirth) took place in the fourteenth, fifteenth, and sixteenth centuries.

After her one thousand years of sleep, Europe awoke and began to colonize Africa, Asia, and the western hemisphere. The Europeans knew very little about Africa; that is why they referred to it as the Dark Continent. As the Europeans explored Africa and transported its sons and daughters into slavery, Africa came under the complete domination of the powers of Europe. At the Berlin Conference in 1880, the European powers divided up Mother Africa. In essence, this meant that white supremacy and racism must take precedence over everything else; this meant that all the glory that once belonged to Africa, the Moslems, and the black Hebrew Israelites would now be undermined and blotted out. These events and various others clearly drew a demarcation line between Europeans and Africans and a division or wider gap between European Jews and African Hebrew Israelites. Like some other white Europeans, some white Jews began to interpret and write books that were flavored with racism.

The White Jews versus the Black Israelites Controversy

In the year 1969 until the present day, a latent controversy grew in greater proportions about the black Israelites. The controversy centered around the fact that the Jewish community in the United States and the state of Israel denied categorically that the black Hebrew Israelites were culturally connected with the ancient nation Israel and were the descendents of the ancient twelve tribes of Israel. This vehement controversy evolved because of two major events.

The first was a domestic event that manifested itself with the publication of my book *From Babylon to Timbuktu*. The pertinent information of this book relevant to our subject under discussion here is the assertion that the ancient Israelites were black, that they migrated to most parts of Africa, and that

113

these Israelites were transported as slaves to the Americas. The second event was an international one. A group of black Israelites, in 1969, departed from the city of Chicago and landed in Liberia, West Africa. After residing in Liberia a short time, they departed for the land of Israel. When they arrived in Israel, the first, second, and third groups were admitted to the country and given tourist visas, pending a decision on their permanent status. Tourist visas are temporary permits that can be renewed at any time, depending on the discretion of the government. The black Israelites claimed that they were bonafide descendants of Israel; the government claimed that they were "not Jews" but blacks pretending to be "Jews." Moreover, the Orthodox rabbis control the portfolio of immigration to the land of Israel, and they maintained that the black Israelites must undergo formal conversion in order to acquire permanent citizenship. This the Israelites refused to do, asserting that "we are already Israelites, and there is no need to convert." The state of Israel and the black Israelites are now deadlocked, neither side budging one bit. I recognize the fact that rabbinical, talmudic law states that a Jew is one who has a Jewish mother or one that converts to Judaism. According to this rationale, if the mother was not Jewish or if she cannot prove her Israelite background through established records or witnesses, any offspring cannot be Jewish; this is talmudic law based on the Torah or the Hebrew scriptures.

Some people might ask from what book of Hebrew scriptures the black rabbis derived their conclusions about the Jewish mother. It is written in Ezra 9:13 and 10:11 that the Jews had taken Canaanite and Moabite wives and had children by some of them. Ezra, the rabbi, and Nehemiah rebuked the Jews and commanded them to put away their strange wives. Why? Because the wives and the mothers of the children were not Jews (Israelites), the wives had not converted to the Jewish religion, the children had not been reared in

114

the Hebrew religion, and the children spoke in the language of their mothers and could not speak in the Jews' language (Hebrew—read Nehemiah 13:23–25). As a consequence of events in the day of Ezra and Nehemiah, they enforced the law of the taking of strange wives and made it crystal clear that any children from those illegal unions were not Israelites or Jewish, because the mother had not converted. The reasoning on a broader level is this: The mother is with the children most of the time. She teaches and trains them; whatever the mother is, the children will be also.

There is a case in the book of Ruth wherein the Israelite Boaz married a Moabite woman. Was this marriage legal? Yes, it was. The Moabite woman, Ruth, converted. She said to Naomi, "Entreat me not to leave thee, or to return from following after thee: for whither thou goest, I will go; and where thou lodgest, I will lodge: thy people shall be my people, and thy God my god." These words of Ruth show her first step toward her complete conversion: a willing heart.

As regards Ezra, he was a priest, a scribe, and a lawyer; the scribes in his days were interpreters and recorders of the law. By the time 168 B.C., the scribes had developed into the Pharisees; the word for Pharisees in Hebrew is *Pirushim*, meaning "Interpreters of the law." The Pharisees also were called *rabbis*, which means "teachers of the law" or "judges."

Now, getting back to the rabbis, I have no fight against talmudic law. In fact, the Talmud was compiled by the black Israelite-scribes and rabbis between the years 500 B.C. and A.D. 500; However, my fight is aginst the interpretation of the law rendered by certain narrow-minded white racist rabbis who interpreted Hebrew law in the strict sense, rather than in the sympathetic, open-minded sense, in light of the prophecies and historical facts that shape modern conditions.

These historical facts are detailed in my first book, *From Babylon to Timbuktu*, and the reader is advised to consult it.

In short, this book describes the migrations of the ancient Israelites to most parts of Africa. There, the European captured them and transported them to America. On the other hand, there are the prophecies of the twenty-eighth chapter of Deuteronomy and others, which I explained earlier in the chapter on curses. According to these curses, many of the Israelites were supposed to lose their country, history, dignity, power, language, culture, traditions, and family connections. Let me explain a prophetic verse from Deuteronomy 28:32 in order to make a relevant point about the loss of family connections; this verse reads as follows: "Thy sons and thy daughters shall be given unto another people and thine eyes shall look, and fail with longing for them all the day long: and there shall be no might in thine hands [to save them]."

Now these white rabbis want the black Israelites to submit family records to prove that they are Israelites. Now tell me how in the world can black Israelites possess written family records when a son and a daughter were sold as slaves to different masters hundreds of miles aparts and it was illegal for a slave to learn to read or write? It is ridiculous; it is comparable to putting a man's eyes out, then asking him if he can see.

In regard to conversion, it is like confessing that we are not Israelites. It is like endorsing a racist system, with its distortions of the black man's history. Furthermore, we are reclaiming our heritage and returning to the true God. I shall reclaim, but shall not use your term "conversion." Black Israelites own their synagogues, houses of prayer, and temples; they don't need your hypocritical conversions. The creator God said, "And it shall come to pass, when all these things are come upon thee, the blessing and the curse, which I have set before thee and thou *shall call them to mind* among all the nations, whither the Lord thy God hath driven thee. And *shall return unto the Lord* thy God, and shall obey his voice

according to all that I command thee this day, thou and thy children, with all thine heart and with all thy soul. That then the Lord thy God will turn thy captivity and have compassion upon thee, and will return and gather thee from all the nations, whither the Lord thy God scattered thee." (Italics are the author's.)

The command of the Creator God to his people is to return unto him; this means to reclaim and return to the law of God. Reclamation is the direction for the Israelites to take, and conversion is for non-Israelites.

Many white Jews will no doubt ask the question "How can you call us racists when we have suffered for centuries? And, recently, we lost six million in the Nazi persecution." Indeed, they have suffered all kinds of prejudice. They should know the feelings of black people who are the victims of prejudice and there should be virtually no prejudice among them. Nevertheless, I have observed the racism among them, and I shall detail more acts of prejudice within Jewish institutions throughout the world, particularly in the state of Israel.

The acts of racism must be exposed. The black Israelites have suffered for thousands of years until now; the black people are suffering in South Africa; the extreme right wing and the Ku Klux Klan are moving throughout America like a tornado. The urgency of the times demand that the voices of militancy and justice be heard; this is not the time for moderation. Let me quote you the words of one of the great abolitionists, William Lloyd Garrison, a white man: "I will be as harsh as truth, and as uncompromising as justice. On this subject [slavery] I do not wish to think, speak, or write with moderation. No! No! Tell a man whose house is on fire to give a moderate alarm; tell him to moderately rescue his wife from the hands of the ravisher; tell the mother to gradually extricate her babe from the fire to which it has fallen; but urge me not to use moderation in a cause like the present! I am in earnest—I will

117

not equivocate—I will not excuse—I will not retreat a single inch—and I will be heard."

Pertaining to the subject of racism, there are various degrees of racists. There are primary or overt racists; these racists don't conceal their thoughts or acts. An example is the Klu Ku Klan. Moreover, there are the secondary or covert racists; sometimes these can be the worst kind, because they are hard to detect, behaving in sly ways. Many white people and some Jews don't shout in public, "Hey, you n——r"; Jews don't advise the incarceration of blacks in concentration camps; Jews don't burn Ku Klux Klan crosses nor lynch black people. In view of this, what is the racism of the Jewish institutions and the government of the state of Israel? This racism is the guilt by gross omission and distortion of the history of the original black Israelites; this racism is guilt by gross neglect of the interest and feeling of black Israelites and simultaneously pretending that the white Jews are the classical friends of the black people in America.

Who Are the Falashas (Ethiopian Black Jews)?

The Falashas, or Ethiopian Jews, were discovered by the European world during the eighteenth and nineteenth centuries, first by James Bruce and then by Joseph Halevy in 1870. Before the white man came to the Falasha country, they never knew that any other white Jews existed and were surprised.

According to the traditions and records of the Falashas, they are the descendants of King Solomon and the Queen of Sheba, through their son Menelik. According to their records, Solomon sent a thousand Hebrews from each of the twelve tribes of Israel to Menelik. They retained the Hebrew culture, and from them the Falashas are descended.

118

Even the former emperor of Ethiopia, Haile Selassie, claimed descent from Menelik, and it is evident that before Christianity came to Ethiopia, there were Jews in Ethiopia.

The Falashas consequently call their religious leaders "priests," in the tradition of the Torah, and strictly follow the Mosaic laws regarding diet, festivals, circumcision, ritual purification, and the Sabbath, which is observed in their synagogues built with the ark for the law and a shield of David (Star of David).

For the past three thousand years, the Falashas have lived as Jews in Ethiopia; this was before any Jews ever lived in Europe. In the third century, they numbered over a million. In the sixteenth century, their number was reduced to five hundred thousand; by the eighteenth century their number had declined to two hundred and fifty thousand; today there are only twenty-five thousand left. Their declining numbers are attributed to disease, poverty, and distress among the young, who are like sharecroppers on Christian land and drifting away from the immediate community in search of jobs. European missionaries for many years have been successfully making the Falasha a special target.

The Persecution of the Black Jews of Ethiopia

Although some sincere white Jews, such as Jacque Faitlovitch, J.I. Fishbein, Dr. Harel, Mario Felsher, and a few other, did a great deal to help the Falashas, much of their efforts and pleading to assist the Falashas in immigrating to the land of Israel fell on deaf ears. The Jewish world, including the state of Israel, said that there was no adequate proof that the Falashas are Jews. Therefore, in the beginning, very little was done to help them.

Whenever a white Jew brought back a report about the

details of Falasha life and history, the white Jewish world asked the question "Are they really Jews?" This was like asking if they could be Jews and black, too. Most of the Jewish world treated the Falasha issue as if they were monkeys in a zoo. By their behavior, the white Jewish world made it plain, by implication, that they could not believe they could be associated with black Jews. But if no one is surprised that a black person is a Christian, then they should not be surprised at a black Jew, because black Jews were in Africa thirteen hundred years before the birth of Christianity. If no one is surprised about a black Muslim, then no one should be surprised about a black Jew, because the black Jews existed in Asia and Africa eighteen hundred years before the birth of Mohammed. When the pope came to America, he visited and accepted the black Catholics. When Muslims from Africa visit Mecca, they are accepted. But some Israelis do not accept black Jews. Since the Ethiopian military regime took power in September of 1974, after the ouster of Emperor Haile Selassie, the Ethiopian Jews have been facing extermination by their own countrymen to a more rapid degree. One young Falasha by the name of Jonas said that Jews were never allowed to own land in Ethiopia and for centuries have been serfs under the feudal landowning system. Now, he said, the regime refuses to extend the agrarian reform to include Falasha ownership of land, with the result that the Falashas are taken into slavery or murdered. He reported that some 2,000 Falashas fled from their villages to avoid being sold into slavery, but many more could not escape this fate.

Jonas also describes atrocities against Falashas, including the raping of young girls in front of their parents and forcing young girls to work as slaves for several families at the same time. He also recited the case of a Jewish woman whose breast was cut off to prevent her nursing her infant.

After one hundred years of procrastination, the white

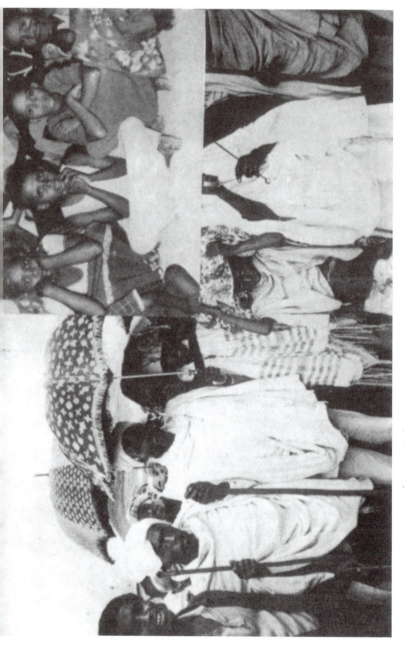

Ethiopian Hebrews in their homeland of Africa. They have lived there for 3,000 years and were living there long before there were any organized nations in Europe.

Jewish rabbis finally recognized the Falashas as bona fide Jews in 1975. In January of 1979, a group of three hundred Falashas demonstrated outside Premier Begin's office, complaining that the "Israeli government and the Zionist institutions were doing too little to rescue Ethiopian Jews. For thirty years, we have waited patiently for action to be done, but to no avail."[2] As is now known, the Israelis then began the secret airlift of Ethiopian Jews to Israel.

The Jewish agency rejected charges by the Falashas that it (the Jewish agency) had acted with indifference to the plight of the Ethiopian Jews. The agency made it clear that it felt restricted, for obvious reasons, from publicizing its efforts on behalf of the Falashas and, therefore, could not address itself to the charges in full. Moreover, Begin appealed to the Falashas to maintain a low profile in their current campaign on behalf of their fellow Falashas still in Ethiopia.

The Israel government claimed that it was not unconcerned about the plight of the Falashas. However, are there any counterviews concerning this issue? Yes! We have the distinguished, respectable Dr. Graenum Berger, a white Jew, who differs with the Jewish authorities. He said that the twenty-eight thousand Falashas "are facing extermination because of the indifference of the Jewish world. This is true for Israel and the Jewish agency, and strangely, it is also true for the American Jewish leadership, which has always been concerned with the plight of black non-Jews."[3] Dr. Berger could be considered an authority on the problem of Ethiopian Jews; he was founder and president of the American Association for Ethiopian Jews.

If the Jewish establishment is not bias, then how does one answer the following questions?

1. Why didn't they invite the Falashas or other dark-skinned Jews to the meeting of the World Zionist Organi-

zation, which began in 1897?

2. Why did the Jewish establishment take 100 years to recognize the Falashas as Jews?

Andrew Young versus the White Jews

For many years, it has been the continuous, relentless policy of the world Jewish community to expedite the emigration of Jews from Russia. The Jewish organizations in this country have employed the power of their abundant money and political clout in the highest office of this land to secure the emigration of the Jews from Russia. One special incident is worth mentioning.

During the Carter administration, a unique episode ensued concerning two Russian dissidents, Anatoly Scharansky and Alexander Ginsberg. The Russian government had indicted these Jews for political crimes against the state. The Jewish world, particularly in the United States, organized a swift challenge against the indictments, the news media gave almost daily reports about the trials, and the Jews in the United States procured the assistance of President Carter and his secretary of state, Cyrus Vance.

At that time, a reporter asked Andrew Young, while he was in Europe, about the Russian Jewish political prisoners. He replied that there were many black political prisoners lingering in the American jails. Almost the entire nation, especially the whites, took offence at his statement; they accused Andy of saying the wrong thing at the wrong time. To them, it was the wrong time, because the American government was negotiating with the Russians for the release of the Jewish political prisoners.

Another fact that give a clear indication of the racism of the Ashkenazi Jews is that the chief Ashkenazi rabbi, Shlomo

Goren, and other state officials who control the government did not recognize the Falashas as bonafide Jews until 1975. However, the chief Sephardic Rabbi, Ovadia Yosef, leader of the Afro-Asian Jews, recognized the Falashas in 1973, in spite of the fact that the Sephardic Jew has very little control in the government. This condition attests to the fact that educational, cultural, social, racial, and political division exist in the Jewish world and in Israeli society.

Two Israeli Societies

Recognizing the fact that social and political division exist in the Jewish world and in the Israeli society, do we have any historical and prophetic material that predicted this condition?

First of all, after the death of King Solomon in the tenth century B.C., the ancient nation of Israel was divided into two separate political entities. The northern kingdom, consisting of ten tribes, was called Israel and the southern kingdom, consisting of one tribe, was called Judah (I Kings 11:29–32). In I Kings 12:19, we learn that the northern kingdom rebelled against the house of David in Judah; furthermore, we learn that Jeroboam, the king of Israel, established two pagan national shrines—one in Bethel, and the other in Dan—in order to divert the loyalty of the ten tribes from Jerusalem (in Judah) to pagan sites in the northern kingdom. King Jeroboam did not want his subjects to recognize the kingdom of Judah, and there was great bitterness between the two kingdoms.

The Israeli government today represents this ancient kingdom of Israel in a symbolical sense, just as the United States represents modern Babylon, the persecutor of the Afro-Israelites. As an inspired researcher, I have numerous reasons to support my contention: Israelites/Jews or Hebrews are supposed to be a divided people until the latter days (the coming

124

of the Messiah, the son of David.) The modern-day state of Israel represents the ancient northern kingdom of Israel for these reasons: The present Israel has the same name as the ancient kingdom of Israel, ancient Israel was located in the northern part of Palestine, the first Jews who returned to the state of Israel in modern time came from mainly European countries, which are in the north, the vast majority of the Sephardic or nonwhite Jews came from Afro-Asian countries, which are in the south, and the Afro-Asian Jews represent the ancient southern kingdom of Judah, which was in the southern section of Palestine. The ancient northern kingdom of Israel rebelled against the southern kingdom of Judah. The ancient kingdom of Israel directed the loyalty of their people from the kingdom of Judah so that they would not recognize the kingdom of Judah. The parallel today is that it is the tendency of many Israelis (northern kingdom and Europeans) is to feel superior to the Afro-Asian Jews, who are represented under the ancient southern kingdom of Judah. Most Jews from the ancient kingdom of Judah fled into Africa.

During the duration of two thousand years of exile and captivity, the European Jews and the Afro-Asian Jews moved wider and wider apart. They became separated geographically, culturally, racially, and idealogically. European Jews thought like Europeans, and Afro-Asian Jews thought like Afro-Asians, as they should have thought, because Israel is in the Afro-Asian world, not in Europe. The prophets foresaw and mentioned the long-continued division between European Jews and Afro-Asian Judeans when they spoke of the two ideological and political units: Judah and Israel. This is what the Lord said by the mouth of Jeremiah, the prophet: "And I will cause the captivity of Judah and the captivity of Israel to return and I will build them as at the first" (Jeremiah 33:7).

There are two separate cultural and political units mentioned throughout the Hebrew Scriptures, and Judah is always

distinct from Israel. Other places where these distinctions are found are Jeremiah 50:4, Joel 3:1–2, Jeremiah 33:16, Isaiah 11:12, Ezekiel 37:16, and Hosea 11:12. When I visited Israel some years ago, I recognized these distinctions. I saw Jews from India who were blacker than any African; these black Jews have some problems with white Jews. Other Afro-Asian Judeans had to organize themselves in order to fight discrimination. One such organization was the Panthers, modeled after the Black Panthers in the United States, who were extremely militant in the 1960s. The Panthers in Israel were not associated with the Black Panthers in the United States, but they told me that they identified and sympathized with the struggle of the black people in the United States.

Another fact that indicates the cultural division in Israel is that many European Jews are very concerned that Israel will become more and more eastern in culture rather than European. These Jews forget that Judaism developed in the Afro-Asian world, not Europe.

Moreover, the cultural division in the state of Israel was so enormous that the situation required the establishment of two separate chief rabbis; as I have mentioned before, one chief rabbi is leader of the Afro-Asian Judeans, representing the kingdom of Judah, and the other chief rabbi is the leader of the European Jews, representing the ancient kingdom of Israel, as I wrote earlier.

The Unity of Jews and Israelites

Although there has been deep division between European Jews and Afro-Asian Israelites, the prophets predicted that there would be harmony and unity in the latter days, at the time of the coming of the Messiah, the son of David. The Lord God said to Ezekiel:

Moreover, thou son of man, take thee one stick, and write upon it, for Judah, and for the children of Israel his companions: then take another stick, and write upon it, for Joseph, the stick of Ephraim, and for all the house of Israel his companions: And join them one to another into one stick; and they shall become one in thy hand. And when the children of thy people shall speak unto thee, saying, wilt thou not show us what thou meaneast by these? Say unto them, thus saith the lord God; Behold, I will take the stick of Joseph, which is in the hand of Ephraim, and the tribe of Israel his fellows and will put them with him, even with the stick of Judah, and make them one stick, and they shall be one in mine hand. Ezekiel 37:16–19

Now, let me explain the symbolism of the two sticks; these sticks represent the two separate divisions of the Jews and the Israelites. God commanded Ezekiel to write on one stick the name of the tribe and kingdom of Judah (Afro-Asian Israelites). In the sixteenth verse, the phrase "the children of Israel his companions" refer to those Israelites who resided within the borders of the kingdom of Judah (II Chronicles 10:17). The Creator God commanded Ezekiel to write on the second stick the name of the tribe of Ephraim for Joseph; Ephraim was the son of Joseph (Genesis 48:1). Furthermore, Ephraim became founder of the ruling tribe and capitol of the northern kingdom of Israel (I Kings 12:19–25). In fact, Ephraim is the nickname of the northern kingdom of Israel; many verses in the Hebrew scriptures confirm this fact. (Read Hosea 5:9.)

Now, we understand that the creator God is going to take the two sticks symbolizing the two kingdoms including the European Jews and the Afro-Asian Israelites and make them one in his hand; this means that he will unite all of these Jews, Hebrews, and Israelites. Then they shall be one nation, not two nations; they shall be one people, not two people (Ezekiel 37:22). For three thousands years, they were separated by

127

hatred, jealousy, and racism, but the Creator God will change all this when he sends the Messiah, the son of David. In the "Latter days," one shepherd or righteous leader will rule over all the Jews, Israelites, and Hebrews. There will not be two chief rabbis in the state of Israel as there are today (Ezekiel 37:2, 3–24). But this day has not arrived yet, and conditions will get worse before they get better.

Notes

1. Lerone Bennett, Jr., *Before the Mayflower* (New York: Penguin Books, Inc. 1966), 188.
2. *Jewish Exponent*, January 12, 1979, Philadelphia, Pennsylvania.
3. *Jewish Exponent*, January 5, 1979, Philadelphia, Pennsylvania.

5

World War III
and Its Secret Cause

World War III will take place in the Middle East. On the human level of understanding, most people believe that the cause of this war will concern the control of the oil fields, but there is a divine hidden reason for the cause of this war of which many people throughout the world are not aware. In this topic, I shall enumerate various scriptural prophesies to support my position.

For more than thirty years, there has been constant warfare and intermittent terroristic acts between the Arabs and the Jewish state. The Middle East will be a boiling pot of conflict for many years to come. There existed an Israelite nation in Palestine (Israel) about 1200 B.C. up to A.D., 70 when the Black Judean state was destroyed by the European Romans. There existed a black Israelite state in the land of Israel for about 1200 years before the rise of Islam, and there were over 3 million black Israelites scattered throughout the Middle East, including Arabia, before the birth of the prophet Muhammed in A.D. 570. In view of this fact, most Arabs do not recognize the right of the existence of an Israelite nation in Palestine. This is one of the prime reasons for the constant conflict in this part of the world: The Arabs do not want a Judean state in the Middle East.

The state of Israel is not the enemy of the Arab states; the enemy of the Arab people is Russia, and time will prove this. The Israelites only want to live in their ancient home in Israel; that is all. But the Russians want to dominate the entire Arab world. The Russian invasion of Afghanistan is just the beginning. The more the Arabs wage war against the state of Israel, the more obligated they are to the Russians for moral support, economic aid, and military weapons. In the not-so-distant future, when the Arabs attack Israel again, the Russians will mobilize their troops and move them into the Middle East under either the disguise of helping the Arabs against the state of Israel or that of protecting the Arab oil fields against European invasion. Eventually, the Russians will act like an occupying imperialist power, controlling the Arab states for her own interest. We shall deal with this subject more extensively later.

Now, in the first paragraph, I mentioned that there is a divine hidden reason for the cause of World War III. The Creator God seeks to summon the various nations to converge down in Palestine in order for them to destroy each other.

Why does the Divine Creator want to destroy the various nations? The answer is because of the multiplicity of crimes that some of the nations committed against the African Israelites. The Creator said these words: "For behold, in those days and in that time when I shall bring again [restore] the captivity of Judah and Jerusalem, I will also gather all nations and will bring them down into the valley of Jehoshophat, and will plead with them there for my people and my heritage Israel, whom they have scattered among the nations and parted my land" (Joel 3:1–2).

Let me explain this verse. What does it mean, in those days and in that time? This mean the latter days, the future days when the Creator of the Heavens and the Earth will restore the Israelites to their own land after a protracted period

of slavery and exile. There is one important point to remember. That is the fact that the restoration of the Israelites is not a one-day event, but a continuous process, spanning decades: "When I shall bring again the captivity of Judah and Jerusalem." Judah was the name of the last black Israelite state that existed during the time of the Babylonian, Persian, Greek, and Roman empires; moreover, Jerusalem was the capitol. The Judeans were captured and sold into slavery by three of the above-mentioned empires. America and Western Europe are racial and cultural extensions of the ancient Roman Empire. Furthermore, the United States and various other nations are guilty of seizing tens of thousands of Black Israelites from the continent of Africa and selling them as slaves. Judah and Jerusalem refer mostly to the non-European or black Israelites of Asia, Africa, and the Americas.

At the time that the Creator God will seek to restore the African Israelites to the land of Israel, he will assemble all nations (political and military blocs) and bring them down to a place in Israel that will be called Jehoshaphat or Armageddon. In this place, the Creator will contend and judge the nations, including Israel, whose people have been scattered and persecuted among the nations and divided up the land called Israel (Joel 3:2).

The Judgment of the Lord

The Creator will bring various power blocs to the land of Israel; these nations will marshal their armies in order to establish control over the holy city of Jerusalem, the oil fields, and the strategic military areas. The desire for control over these locations will provoke different power blocs to fight each other for the mastery of this region. The Divine Creator will

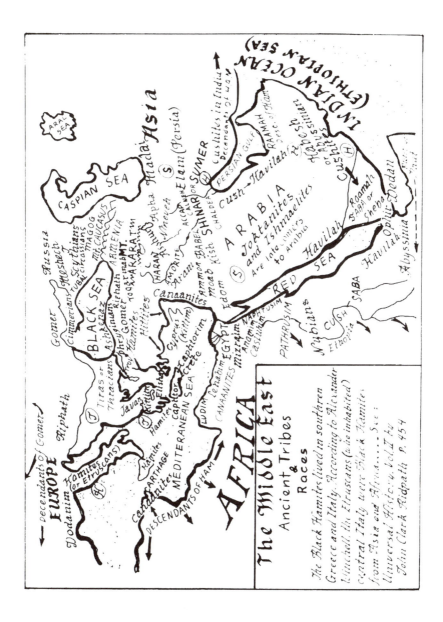

use the oil, the various holy shrines in Jerusalem, and the strategic location of Israel as bait in a trap to accomplish his purpose; his purpose is the restoration of the Israelites and the destruction of the wicked nations. (Nations have always gone to war to satisfy their national interests.)

The prophet Joel said in his book, 3:9: "Proclaim ye this among the Gentiles; Prepare war, wake up the mighty men, let all the men of war, draw near; let them come up: Beat your plowshares into swords . . . let the weak say, I am strong." What does it mean to "beat your plowshares . . . "? This sentence means "Convert your farming equipment into military weapons so that you can prepare for war." Today, most Third World countries don't have running water piped into their homes, but their governments possess some of the most-sophisticated weapons in their war arsenals. Yes, the first stage is set. The nations are preparing for war, not peace; the decision has gone forth from the Almighty God.

> Assemble yourselves, and come all ye heathen, and gather yourselves together round about [near Jerusalem] thither cause thy mighty ones to come down O Lord.
>
> Joel 13:11

The mighty ones are the ministering angels of the Creator God; they will direct the war action at Armageddon and will bring about the destruction of the wicked (II Samuel 24:15, 16; II Kings 19:35). Moreover, the angel reassured Gideon that the Lord would be with him, because the angel was permitted by the Creator to assist Gideon and direct the outcome of the battle. Judges 6:11–12: "Let the heathen [non-Jews] be awakened and come up to the valley of Jehoshaphat: for there will I sit to judge all the heathen round about." Why land how will God judge the nations that marshal their armies at Jerusalem? I shall answer the "Why" first:

> And they have cast lots for my people; and have given a boy for an harlot and sold a girl for wine that they might drink the

133

children also of Judah and the children of Jerusalem have ye sold unto the Grecians that ye might remove them far from their border. (Joel 3:3–6)

In the days of the prophet Joel, the ancient people of Lebanon known as Zedonians and Palestinians sold the Jews into slavery and wherever the Judeans migrated, the gentiles persecuted them.

How will the Lord judge the nations? We must be aware of the fact that there is no judgment without a sentence or punishment. The trial of the wicked is held in the heavenly court, but the sentence is meted out on earth. Many large opposing armies will converge in the Middle East for their own selfish interest, and there they will receive their sentence of destruction (Zechariah 12:2–9; 14:2,3). The prophet Zechariah describeds in vivid detail the most horrible destruction that the various nations will unleash on one another when God brings them against Jerusalem: "And this shall be the plague where with the Lord will smite all people that have fought against Jerusalem; their flesh shall consume away while they stand upon their feet, and their eyes shall consume away in their holes and their tongue shall consume away in their mouth."

What is this unusual kind of destruction that takes place while a man stands on his feet? In conventional warfare, a man is shot or blown up by artillery shells and usually falls down almost immediately. On the other hand, the prophet Zechariah describes a destruction, a plague, a consumption or wasting away of the body that is worse than leprosy, smallpox, and gangrene combined, because the flesh and organs deteriorate and fall away as a man is walking. The gruesome description indicated here can be of nothing else but the results of the explosion of the atomic bomb, causing the release of nuclear radiation. There is no hiding place on the surface of the earth from the nuclear fallout; the innocent near

and far are "plagued" by it. The scientists say there are two important facts about the nature of radiation: it cannot be detected by the human sense organs, and it is very difficult to block.

The Russian Invasion of the Middle East

Yes! The Union of the Soviet Socialist Republics, also known as Russia, will invade and occupy the Middle East. My statement is confirmed by many biblical scholars. Everyday biblical prophecy is being fulfilled before our very eyes. This fact lends itself to the authenticity of the Hebrew scriptures as one of the most inclusive and accurate holy books in existence. Now, let a multiplicity of evidence speak for itself.

The word of the Creator God came unto Ezekiel, the prophet, around the year 585 B.C.:

> Son of man, set thy face against Gog, the land of Magog, the chief prince of Meshech and Tubal, and prophesy against him.
> Ezekiel 38:2

It is necessary to identify these ancient names in order to obtain a geographical indication of their location; therefore, a knowledge of ancient history is highly important to understanding the Bible. The word "Gog" appears to be a title of a leader of the people in the land of Magog, Meshech, and Tubal. The latter three names are mentioned in Genesis 10:2 among the sons of Japheth.

Josephus, the historian, informs us that the Scythians descended from the Magogites. *Webster's Geographical Dictionary* reveals that Scythia was the ancient name of parts of Southern Europe and Asia now included in Russia; the Scythians were a nomadic and savage race that inhabited regions north and northeast of the Black Sea and east of the Aral Sea

in Southern Russia. Also, Josephus indentifies the word *Meshech* with the word *Mosoch*, which is *Moscow*, the capital of the Soviet Union, another way of saying *Moscow* is *Muscovy*. Josephus said that the descendants of Tubal were the Iberians who resided between the Black and Caspian Seas. Many of these people migrated northward and fixed some of their ancient names on towns and rivers. There is the Tobal River (Tubal) in Central Russia. It is eight hundred miles long and rises in the southeastern foothills of the Ural Mountains and flows northeast to the Irtysh River at the town of Tobolsk. This town can only be the same as the ancient name Tubal with a Russianized suffix. Many names on the modern maps of Russia have "sk" for their endings; the Ural mountains are called *Uralsk* in Russian, and so on.

Before I conclude the explanation of this verse, I want to analyse the phrase "Chief prince of," which is found in Ezekiel 38:2. "Chief prince of" is a poor translation of the Hebrew words *Nisi Rosh*, which mean "prince of Rosh." The word "Rosh" should be translated as a proper noun, not an adjective, because in Hebrew the phrase is used in the construct state, which is similar to our English possessive case. The correction is now rendered *nisi Rosh* (prince of Rosh or Russ); this name is that of Russia. My correction makes grammatical, contextual, and historical good sense. Gog is the leader or prince of Rosh (Russia) and Meshech (Moscow), and there is not the slightest doubt in my mind.

Now, we know who these names are; let us see what is the plan of the Creator God for these people.

Thus saith the Lord God; Behold, I am against thee, O Gog, the chief prince [The prince of Russia] of Meshech and Tubal: And I will turn thee back and put hooks into thy jaws, and I will bring thee forth, and all thine army, horses and horsemen, all of them clothed in all sorts of armour, even a great company with bucklers and shields, all of them handling swords.

Ezekiel 38:3–4

It is revealed in the thirty-eighth and thirty-ninth chapters of Ezekiel that the Lord will bring the Russian armies against the land of Israel. These events will materialize in the latter years after the establishment of the State of Israel. At this time, the Jews will be living in a state of security and great wealth. The massive mobilization of the Russian armies will be motivated by greed and desire for world domination. Moreover, other nations will accompany the Russians in their invasion.

> Gomer, and all his bands the house of Togarmah of the North quarters, and all his bands and many people with thee.
>
> Ezekiel 38:6

Eastern Europe

Gomer is mentioned in Genesis 10:2 as the oldest son of Japhet, and most ancient maps show the descendants of Gomer and Togarmah in Northeastern Europe, the north, and central Russia, respectively. Some writers identify the house of Togarmah with certain Turkaman tribes in Central Asia. *Harper's Bible Commentary* says that the offspring of Gomer are the Cimmerians, their original abode was north of the Black Sea and from this location they migrated to various parts of Eastern Europe.

The Northern Army or Bloc

> *And thou shall come from thy place out of the north, thou, and many people with thee, all of them riding upon horses, a great company, and a mighty army.*
>
> *Ezekiel 38:15*

137

The army destined to invade the Middle East and the state of Israel will descend from the north. In fact, in the Hebrew language the text read: "Miyarkitay Tsafon." This mean the extreme or remote north. It does not mean that the army will come from Lebanon, Syria, or Turkey. "The North" means the focal point from the land of Israel, and the only nation to the extreme north of the land of Israel is Russia. Just consider how accurate the prophecy of God is: "Thou shalt ascend and come like a storm, thou shall be like a cloud to cover the land, thou, and all thy bands and many people with thee" (Ezekiel 39:9).

"Thou [referring to Russia] and all thy bands, and many people with thee"—Russia will not be by herself when she invades the Middle East, but with her will be the communist satellite countries of Eastern Europe, which are behind the Iron Curtain. The Communist countries are as follows:

Communist Countries	Population
Soviet Union	262,436,000
Poland	35,227,000
Romania	22,057,000
Yugoslavia	22,174,000
East Germany	16,758,000
Czechoslovakia	15,239,000
Afghanistan *	14,699,000
Hungary	10,710,000

Bulgaria	8,827,000
Lithuania	3,300,000
Latvia	2,521,000
Estonia	1,466,000
Mongolia*	1,616,000
Total	417,000,000

The two countries marked with asterisks are not located in eastern Europe, but they are behind the Iron Curtain.

Mongolia is a country north of China. With the advent of the 1911 Chinese revolution, Mongolia, with Russian backing, declared its independence. A Mongolian communist regime was established in July of 1921.

Mongolia has sided with the Russians in the Sino-Russian dispute. A Mongolian-Soviet mutual-assistance pact was signed on January 15, 1966, and thousands of Soviet troops are based in the country. Ties were expanded in a 1976 pact.

Afghanistan—late in December of 1979, the USSR began a massive airlift of military cargo into Kabul, Afghanistan. The three-month-old regime of Hafizullah Amin terminated with a Soviet-backed coup on December 27. Amin was replaced by Babrak Karmal, considered a more pro-Soviet leader. Soviet troops estimated at between 60,000–100,000 moved throughout the country fighting Afghan rebels.

Now, let us return to Russia, the northern power, "and all thy bands." This Russian power and nation extend across two continents, Europe and Asia; even in Asia, Russia is in the extreme north latitudes. The prophet Ezekiel said, "And

many people with thee." The prophet continues, "Thou shalt ascend and come like a storm, thou shalt be like a cloud to cover the land." This means that when the Russians and her satellites mobilized their armies, navies, and air forces, they would put into the skies thousands of supersonic jets, trooptransport planes, and helicopters. These airships are capable of firing missiles at tremendous speed. The speed of these supersonic jets were so great that the prophet compared them to a storm (tornado), and their numbers were so numerous that the prophet compared them to the clouds that cover the lands.

During World War II, I remember seeing many squadrons of airplanes flying over my hometown. There were so many of them that they seemed like a cloud that covered the ground; also, they produced a shadow by blocking the sunlight. Today, naturally, they have tens of thousands of jets in the communist countries. Imagine what the skies will look like in the impending invasion of the Middle East.

Persia (Iran)

There are other nations who will be allied with the Russians when they invade Israel and the Middle East.

> Persia . . . with them; all of them with shield and helmet.
> Ezekiel 38:5

The ancient name Persia was changed to the name Iran on March 22, 1935. Iran will fall behind the communist Iron Curtain in the near future; it is in prophecy, and make no mistake about the course Iran will take. A communist government may take over at any time. In fact, parts of Iranian territory are already behind the Iron Curtain. In 1857, the British severed the region known as Afghanistan from Iran,

and, as I have mentioned earlier, the Russians dispatched about 100,000 troops into Afghanistan in December of 1979. Not only are the Russians stationed on the northern border of Iran, but with their presence in Afghanistan, they are poised on Iran's eastern border. When Iran falls behind the Iron Curtain, another 37 million people will be added to the communists before I finish this book. Incidentally, some African nations will be allied with the Russians.

Africans

Ethiopia and Libya with them; all of them with shields and helmet.

Ezekiel 38:5

There is every reason to believe that the various African tribes descended from those of Libya and Ethiopia in ancient times. In fact, on maps of Africa that were drawn up by Europeans during the Middle Ages, all of Africa was called Ethiopia. According to the prophet Ezekiel, many African countries will be allied with the Russians when they invade the land of Israel. It is later than many of us think. The stage is already set, and there are actions that have already been set in motion which inevitably will lead up to the horrible war of God's judgement, Armageddon.

There are at the present time a number of states in Africa that are or have been under communist or socialist influence:

Egypt

After the Arab-Israeli War of 1967, Egypt received military and economic aid from the USSR; it was estimated in 1971 that there were nineteen thousand or more Soviet military personnel in Egypt.

In July of 1972, President Sadat ordered most of the

141

Russians to leave; they complied. Nevertheless, some military shipments have continued. During the 1973 Yom Kipur War, Egypt received a military arilift from Russia.

Mali

In 1968, a coup ended the socialist regime.

Mozambique

When the government took over after 1974, the Maoist president, Samora Machel, promised a gradual transition to a communist system.

Libya.

The USSR sold several billion dollars' worth of advanced arms after 1975 and established close political ties with Libya

Algeria

A one-party Socialist regime. In 1967, Algeria declared war with Israel, broke with the U.S. and moved toward eventual military and political ties with the USSR.

Angola

The Soviet-backed popular movement rules the country. There were fifteen thousand Cuban troops and massive Soviet aid that helped the Popular movement win the battles against the National Union, which was backed by the United States and South Africa.

Ethiopia

Now this nation is a one-party socialist state, with close ties to Russia. Relations with the United States have deteriorated; as a result, cooperation accords were signed with the USSR in 1977, In 1978, Soviet advisors and twenty thousand communist Cuban troops helped Ethiopia defeat Somali rebels.

The trend is set, and the nations are moving in the direc-

tion in which the prophecy of God said they would move. Libya and Ethiopia have already moved, as you can see, in this direction, and the rest of Africa will follow as events unfold.

Some of you are probably wondering why some African states would want to turn communist. Obviously, the answers are poverty, greed, racism, and colonialism. I shall give you an indication of the course the African states will take by stating this fact. When Egypt attacked Israel, who was supported by the United States and other Western powers, in the 1973 war, most African states broke diplomatic relations with the state of Israel. It seems highly likely that in any war in which Russia and the Arabs are against Israel and Western Europe, the Africans will be confederates of Russia.

Russian Domination of the Islamic States

Before the Russians attack the state of Israel, an African-Arab bloc of confederate nations will strike against the Israelis. Why? Because the issues of the Palestinians, the West Bank, and Jerusalem appear unsolvable. Moreover, the entire area is being inundated with devastating weapons and the extremists are gaining control on both sides. There will be horrible, horrible consequences unleashed on mankind.

This African-Arab bloc will fall under the leadership of the king of the South. Read the words of Daniel 11:40: "And at the time of the end shall the king of the south push at him."

Who is the king of the South? Remember I told you that the focal point of direction is determined from the land of Israel and geographically Egypt is south of Israel. There is a tremendous amount of historical evidence to certify this point.

Just briefly, let me retrace the historical events in the eleventh chapter of the book of Daniel. After Alexander the Great conquered the entire Middle East and Egypt, his general Seleucus established a dynasty in Syria and became the

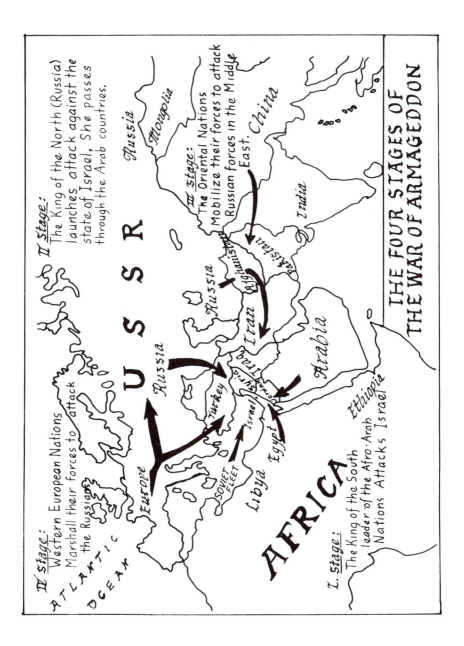

THE FOUR STAGES OF THE WAR OF ARMAGEDDON

II. stage:
The King of the North (Russia) launches attack against the state of Israel. She passes through the Arab countries.

III. stage:
The Oriental Nations Mobilize their forces to attack Russian forces in the Middle East.

IV. stage:
Western European Nations Marshall their forces to attack the Russians.

I. stage:
The King of the South leader of the Afro-Arab Nations Attacks Israel.

144

king of the north, and his other general, Ptolemy, established a dynasty in Egypt and became the king of the south. Daniel did not designate these kings by names, but only referred to them as the king of the north and the king of the south during the time that the Greeks dominated the Middle East. You can read about the details and events of this period in the writings of Josephus and the books of the Apocrypha. During the time that the Greeks ruled, there was constant war between Syria and Egypt, and this is what Daniel is talking about in most of the eleventh chapter. Then, all of a sudden, Daniel jumped over 2,000 years to our day in verse 11:40, and he said, "At the time of the end." What is the time of the end? It is the latter days when the Creator God will judge the wicked nations, after the establishment of the state of Israel, and bring their armies to the war of Armageddon in Israel. In the Fortieth verse, Daniel expressly reveals to us that the King of the South (Egypt, Arabs, and other Africans) will push at "him" (Israel). This means that the Arab-African bloc will attack the state of Israel. At this time, Israel will be supported by the United States and Western Europe or one of the two.

And the king of the north shall come against him [the Israeli head of state] like a whirlwind, with chariots and with horsemen, and with many ships and he shall enter into the countries, and shall overflow and pass over.

We have learned in this chapter that the king of the north is Russia, and when the African-Arab confederacy attacks Israel, the Russians will move against the state of Israel like a whirlwind, with chariots (tanks) and many divisions of troops. Thousands of supersonic jets will sound like a whirlwind. If the Russians do not participate actively in the next Arab-Israeli war, then they will in the subsequent wars.

The Nature of the Russian Armed Forces

"The king of the north will come against him like a whirlwind." Daniel, the man of God, conveys to us the point that the Russians will be vigorously decisive in their aggression. That is, they will not hesitate, for they come like a whirlwind with armored divisions and with a mighty naval fleet. At this time, let me explore the character and potential of the Russian armed forces, especially their naval power.

First of all, the United States of America is no longer a first-rate power in the world, but Russia is. The Russians know this very well; this is the main reason they will not hesitate. (Remember the invasion of Afghanistan.) The chief of staff of the United States Army, Edward C. Meyer, said, in short, that the American military capability comparable to Russia is a sad saga.

Military and other specialists believe that the ultimate aim of the Russians is to sever the sea lanes by which the Western World transports important minerals.

The Soviet Union has no overseas territory or military bases that must be supplied by her navy; however, in certain parts of the Third World, some might be under construction. Because she does not rely on foreign imports, she has no necessity to fear a sea blockade. Moreover, the USSR is virtually unsusceptible to invasion by her coastline, because her beaches are either too difficult to assault or too far away from any vital military goal.

Nevertheless, Soviets possess in excess of 2,025 vessels in her fleet; this is about four times greater than the United States possesses. Russia has more destroyers, cruisers, and submarines than the United States. Russian vessels, at this time, are much more heavily armed and generally faster, and the Russians use a larger quantity of short-range missiles on their assault ships.

Listen to this so called "secret report," as revealed on "The Phil Donahue Show" in April 1981, by Congressman Clarence Long (a Democrat from Maryland). He said, "The United States is behind the Russians in every category, and this includes quantity and quality." The Russians control the land, the air, and the seas.

Daniel saw the Russian military forces moving toward the land of Israel and toward other Muslim countries in "many ships," and this northern power has the mightiest navy in the world today. It is crystal clear that Daniel foresaw that Russia poses the greatest danger to the Muslim countries, and this danger is not the state of Israel.

> He shall enter also into the glorious land, and many countries shall be overthrown: but these shall escape out of his hand, even Edom, and Moab and the chief of the children of Ammon.
>
> Daniel 11:41

In the latter part of the fortieth verse, Daniel said that Russia would "enter into the countries and shall overflow and pass over." With the invasion of the Muslim country of Afghanistan, the first stage of this process has already begun, make no mistake about it! We are now living in the time period of Armageddon, and the process will move from stage to stage until the main event ends with a worldwide holocaust.

Again, Daniel tells us that the Soviet Union will "enter also into the glorious land" (forty-first verse). The glorious land is the land of Israel. I had mentioned earlier to you that the prophet Ezekiel said that the Creator God would bring this northern power, Russia, against the land of Israel. According to Ezekiel, the Russians will come to the land of Israel to spoil and rob the country of its wealth. Right now, a country without oil fields, Israel, with a population of under 4 million, has a gross national product of $16 billion, compared to Jordan,

147

a country with about the same population, with only a gross national product of $2 billion. Furthermore, Israel's discoveries of potash (a potent fertilizer) in the Dead Sea are of significant worth trillions of dollars; that is a lot of wealth for a small country.

"Many countries shall be overthrown"—Daniel, here, is referring to various Muslim countries that surround the state of Israel. Some will be conquered; other will be forced to submit to Russian communist domination. According to Daniel, in the forty-first verse, the countries that will escape the harsh treatment of Russia are only Edom, Moab, and Ammon. These countries were located on the east side of the Jordan River, and today they compose the modern nation of Jordan. Amman is the capital of Jordan and gets its name from the ancient nation of Ammon. Why will Jordan escape from Russian hands? There are several reasons: She is not a very rich country; she has no oil fields and very few minerals. Moreover, Jordan has no real strategic military value. She is a landlocked country and has very little coastline.

> He shall stretch forth his hand also upon the countries and the land of Egypt shall not escape. But he [Russia] shall have power over the treasures of gold and of silver, and over all the precious things of Egypt: and the Libyans and the Ethiopians shall be at his steps.

Although Jordan escapes the cruel hand of Russia, Egypt will not escape and the remainder of the Muslim countries will fall like dominos under the Russian bear hug. Why is it that Daniel singles out the Muslim country of Egypt? The heart and nerve center of the Arab world is Egypt. She has the largest Arabic-speaking population, over 40 million people. Anyone that has a little knowledge of geography and history would recognize the fact that any Russian control of the Middle East would be predicated on the domination of Egypt. When

Egypt falls to the Russians, they will have complete control of the economy, commerce, and destiny of Egypt; the economy of a country is a people's lifeline. Daniel says that "he [Russia] shall have power over the treasures of gold and silver and over all the precious things of Egypt." Furthermore, Daniel singles Egypt out for complete conquest, because Russia will have a vital need for the Egyptian harbors and the Suez Canal. The Suez Canal has great economic and military value; it connects the three great continents of Europe, Africa, and Asia. Russia will be in a strategic, advantageous position to stop and stangulate the oil windpipe of Western Europe.

"And the Libyans and the Ethiopians shall be at his steps"—Considering the pertinent prophecies, history, and current events, I believe that this quotation about Libya and Ethiopia means that most African states will become socialist or will maintain close ties with the Soviet Union. As I have mentioned earlier, two key African states have already joined the Soviet camp. They are Angola and Ethiopia. When you look at the map of Africa, you can realize the important geographical position of Ethiopia. In order for ships to enter the Suez Canal via the Red Sea from the Indian Ocean, they must first enter the straits of bar El Mandeb. This narrow waterway separates South Yemen from Ethiopia, and unfriendly ships could be prevented here from entering the Suez Canal by Russian or Ethiopian armed forces.

Moreover, the Soviet-backed government in Angola (southwest Africa) could permit the Russians to construct a naval base in that country. If this happens, the Soviets would be in a beneficial position to prevent the shipping of oil around the Cape of Good Hope and the export of vital minerals from racist South Africa to Europe and the United States. Watch for more Russian activity in the Middle East and Africa. At this writing, South Yemen, a country in southern Arabia, has already fallen under communist rule.

149

But remember, after the Arab-African bloc attacks the state of Israel, the Russians will initiate a massive land, sea, and air attack against the state of Israel in order to exploit the wealth of the country. Obviously, this move is intended to make the Arabs look favorably on the Russians. But, as time passes, the probability is that the Russians will double-cross the Arabs and become the new imperial masters of the Middle East.

> But tidings out of the East and out of the North shall trouble him: therefore he [Russia] shall go forth with great fury to destroy, and to take away many.

At this point, the Russian military commander receives a communiqué that the Oriental (yellow) races are mobilizing forces in the Far East. China has a population of over a billion people and an army of 200 million troops. As the Russian forces are entrenched in the Middle East, they also hear unfavorable news from the north. By the north, here Daniel is referring to the power bloc that is located in northwestern Europe and known as the North Atlantic Treaty Organization. (Notice the word *north* in this European organization.) The European economic community or the Common Market, is the classical name for these ten noncommunist European nations. These ten nations are Belgium, Denmark, France, West Germany, Ireland, Italy, Luxembourg, the Netherlands, the United Kingdom, and Greece. These ten nations represent the ten toes or ten horns spoken by Daniel in Daniel 2:41 and 7:7. The Common Market nations are nothing but the revival of the ancient Roman Empire; they have already moved in the direction of a common economy, a common monetary system, a common immigration and passports, and they are moving rapidly toward a common political system including coordination of military forces. Because of the weakness of

the United States, the Western Europeans are moving toward integration and unification of their various nations in order to be strong enough to meet the Soviet challenge. It is no doubt that Germany, with a gross national product of over $700 billion, will play the major role in this new European empire. And the total Common Market gross national product is around $2,000 billion. This is a lot of economic and military power needed in order to be prepared to meet the Russians in the Middle East.

We must not forget that although man has his terrestrial and greedy purpose for waging war, the Creator God has his masterplan designed in advance for all humanity. One of his purposes is to bring the wicked nations together for judgment and destruction in the war of Armageddon or the war of Jehoshaphat (this word means the judgement of the Lord). In Joel 3:3, the prophet gives two principal reasons why the Creator God shall bring the armies of the nations into World War III to meet their destruction. First of all, they have scattered and dispersed the original black Hebrew Israelites among the nations into captivity and slavery. Second of all, the nations have parted or divided the land of Israel for their own gain. According to some interpretations of the Book of Daniel, 11:39–45, the leader of the Common Market nations will partition the land of Israel in the not-too-distant future; this act will spark World War III, and the Arab-African bloc will attack the state of Israel (fortieth verse).

The world is divided into four main power blocs, and this is confirmed in Daniel 11:40–45: (1) The king of the south (the Arab-African bloc); (2) the king of the north (Russia and her satellites); (3) the east (China and her satellites); and (4) the north or Northwest Europe (including the United States, Canada, and all the white Christian nations that derived from Europe).

Now, let me return to the central point in order to con-

tinue the dramatic events with the Russian occupation of the Middle East. In the forty-fourth verse of the book of Daniel, we learn that the Russian army commander hears the bad news that the Chinese and the European Common Market forces are moving toward the Middle East. All the armies of the nations and of mankind are brought down by the Creator God to the inferno of the Middle East. In Joel 3:14, it says: "Multitudes, multitudes in the valley of decision." It appears to me, by my analysis of the prophecies, that Armageddon is not a one-day or one-month affair, but a series of events extending over years with the destruction of certain power blocs, then followed by a pause in hostilities, then, again, followed by the resumption of international conflict with terrible slaughter.

> Behold, I will make Jerusalem a cup of trembling unto all the people round about, when they shall be in the siege both against Judah and Jerusalem. In that day, I will make Jerusalem a burdensome stone for all people: All that burden themselves with it shall be cut in pieces, though all the people of the earth be gathered against it.
>
> Zechariah 12:2, 14:2

In the forty-fourth verse, we learn that the Russian prepare themselves to fight "with great fury" against the Chinese and the Western European nations. Many of the battles take place in the Middle East and around Jerusalem.

> And he [Russia] shall plant the tabernacles of his palace [headquarters] between the seas in the glorious holy mountain; yet he shall come to his end, and none shall help him.
>
> Daniel 11:45

Evidently, the Russians shall move their forces and headquarters from North Africa (see Daniel 43) to the glorious holy

mountain (Mount Zion, Jerusalem), which is between the Mediterranean and the Dead Sea. The northern power, Russia, whom Ezekiel called Gog and Magog in chapters thirty-eight and thirty-nine will meet his complete destruction. The Creator God uses the Chinese and Western Europeans to unleash weapons of terrible devastation on the Russians; these weapons are supersonic jets firing missiles, surface-to-air missiles, submarine Polaris missiles, and intercontinental ballistic missiles with nuclear warheads. Some of these warheads pack more than 1 million tons of T.N.T. This is the manner in which the prophet Ezekiel described the destruction of the Lord. "And I will plead against him with pestilence and with blood; and I will rain upon him and upon his bands and upon many people that are with him, and over-flowing rain, and great hailstones, fire, and brimstones" (Ezekiel 38:22).

By pestilence, the prophet obviously meant massive horrible deaths by nerve gas, germ warfare, and nuclear radiation. We need to examine the phrase "rain upon him" and "an overflowing rain, and great hailstones, fire, and brimstones." I doubt that the Creator is referring to natural rain and hailstones; these natural elements could hurt the modern war machines very little. Evidently, the prophet meant that the Creator would rain down rapid massive-firing missiles and other weapons of destruction by fire. The missiles and bombs seemed to the prophet like hailstones and brimstones (balls of fire) falling out of heaven. The prophet had to use words that he knew; in his day, two thousand years ago, tanks, supersonic jets, and missiles were unheard of.

And I will send a fire on Magog, and among them that dwell carelessly in the isles: and they shall know that I am the Lord.
Ezekiel 39:6

The word *isles* refers to distant islands and continents

153

across the seas and oceans. Before the Russians are utterly destroyed, they will get an opportunity to fire their missiles at other nations in the Americas, Europe, Asia, and Africa. In some of these nations across the seas, the people dwell carelessly. That is, they think that they are secure and live a life of ease.

> And it shall come to pass in that day, that I will give unto Gog a place there of graves in Israel, the valley of the passengers on the east of the sea: and it shall stop the noises of the passengers: and there shall they bury Gog and all his multitude: and they shall call it The Valley of Hamon-Gog. And seven month shall the house of Israel be burying of them, that they may cleanse the land.
>
> Ezekiel 39:11–16

Although Russia shall be finished as a world power, Armageddon will not be over. It looks like there will be a lull between the next storm. It seems highly likely that the next phase of the Armageddon conflict will be waged between the western European empire and China.

> And at that time shall Michael stand up, the great prince which standeth for the children of thy people: and there shall be a time of trouble, such as never was since there was a nation even to that same time: and at that time thy people shall be delivered, every one that shall be found written in the book.
>
> Daniel 12:1

The theme in this verse is a time of great trouble. The historians know that all wars and international conflicts are interrelated. The conditions in the world after World War I contributed to World War II, and the conditions in the world after World War II will contribute to World War III. It is a chain reaction. Man's inhumanity to man, greed, selfishness, arrogance, disregard for human life, and the lack of understanding, compassion, and mercy ("There is no truth, nor

154

mercy nor knowledge of God in the land"—Hosea 4:1) will lead all mankind down the road to complete annihilation. We have now approached the brink of Armageddon, and when it comes, nations will slaughter one another on land, on sea, and in the air with maniacal fury. The gruesome weapons that man have created are capable of decimating the planet Earth more than five times. Here are some examples of terrible weapons:

Earthquake stimulation—Mankind has discovered a new way of destroying millions of people; the new technique is accomplished by stimulating earthquake belts.

Chemicals—There are incendiary weapons that produce chemical horrors generating or radiating thermal energy similar to that of the atomic bomb.

Sound reproduction or sound rays—Experimentation has shown that human beings can be totally disoriented by unheard infrasound. If these experiments are perfected, sound rays may be a new weapon for the decimation of mankind.

Nerve Gas—Small amounts of nerve agents (for example, Sarin or VX gas) can wreak unbelievable destruction on unsuspecting millions of people. I am informed that just one canister of the cardinal potency gas is capable of destroying almost 2 billion lives.

The Neutron Bomb—Dissimilar from the H Bomb, the neutron bomb has the capacity to produce a flood of deadly radiation, with no destruction to inanimate objects such as superstructures. The production of these weapons is already complete. And they are agents of silent death.

Germ Warfare—The destruction of entire populations by biological agents such as tularemia, anthrax, melioidosis, brucellas, and Q fever is so highly dangerous that less than twelve ounces if properly disseminated could destroy all humanity.

The major powers of the earth have constructed a ring of nuclear destruction around the world. These powers are

155

the Soviet Union, the United States, France, Great Britain, China, and India. There are some smaller nations believed to have the bomb or the reactors or the potential for making them. Many countries fear that these awful weapons might fall in the hands of terrorist groups, who would use them to blackmail any nation into capitulation. We are all sitting on a time bomb of destruction, and we have no one to blame but ourselves. We are guilty, because we have permitted evil to exist in the world and in our neighborhoods. We have turned the other way, instead of speaking out, and we shall reap the bitter fruit of our unjust doings.

Here are some statements of world leaders and scholars about the survival of mankind:

Former French President Valery Giscard d' Estaing: "The world is unhappy, unhappy because it does not know where it is going and because it guesses that it is going toward a catastrophe."

Bertrand Russell: "Never since human beings first existed have they been faced with so great a danger as that which they have brought upon themselves by a combination of unrivaled skill and unrivaled folly."

Dr. Herbert York: "The arms race is a steady open spiral downward toward oblivion."

Dr. Robert Herbronner: "Nobody is equipped to deal with problems that are rushing in on us, from inflation to nuclear weapons."

Douglas MacArthur: "We have had our last chance. If we will not devise some greater and more equitable system, Armageddon will be at the door."

Henry Kissinger: "The Western world seems to be floating without power or rudder on a sea filled with destructive events."

Albert Einstein: "There is no defense in science against the weapon that can destroy civilization."

We have received the warnings from world leaders and the ancient prophets. Listen to what Jeremiah, the prophet said for our day:

> A noise shall come even to the ends of the earth; for the Lord has a controversy with the nations, he will plead with all flesh; he will give them that are wicked to the sword [destruction], saith the Lord. Thus saith the Lord of hosts, Behold, evil shall go forth from nation to nation and a great whirlwind shall be raised up from the coasts of the earth. And the slain of the Lord shall be at that day [in this generation] from one end of the earth even unto the other end of the earth: they shall not be lamented, neither gathered, nor buried; they shall be dung upon the ground.
>
> Jeremiah 25:31–33

The evil that will go forth from nation to nation is nothing but savage warfare among nations. Moreover, the slain from the nuclear catastrophe will be from one end of the earth to the other, and there will be very few people around to mourn or to bury the dead bodies, and the corpses shall be stinking on the surface of the earth. This is how the Creator judges the wicked nations; "He removeth kings [presidents] and setteth up kings: he giveth wisdom unto the wise and knowledge to them that know understanding" (Daniel 2:21).

During the time of this great catastrophe shall Michael stand up, the great prince which standeth for the children of thy people (and the righteous gentiles) and at this time shall the righteous be delivered. Daniel said that at this time of the end, "Many shall run to and fro and knowledge shall increase." The phrase "run to and fro" means there will be massive rapid transportation from one place to another. "And knowledge shall increase"—this means that there will be many technological advancements; you see, we are living in the

times that Daniel was talking about. We have reached the moon, and the space shuttle *Columbia* circled the earth over thirty times (knowledge shall increase). One reporter asked a woman, "What do you think of the launching of the *Columbia?*" She replied, "It's great. I am proud of America." What is there to be proud of? Thousands are facing starvation around the world, South Africa is on the verge of a racial explosion, and all that the president can say is that we will trade with South Africa but we do not endorse her racial policies. White Catholics and Protestants are fighting one another with a passion; you cannot walk the streets in safety in America, with blacks killing blacks, whites killing whites, and black and whites killing each other, and four people, including the president are shot in Washington, D.C. What is there to be proud of? Again, I shall repeat, we are living in the time that Daniel wrote about: "Many shall be purified and made white, [made righteous] and tried; but the wicked shall do wickedly: none of the wicked shall understand but the wise shall understand."

Many of the wicked who will read my book will not understand it, but they will do ten times more wickedly than before their previous deeds. But the wise and righteous will understand.

Salvation Is of the Jews

There are numerous indications throughout the entire Bible to support the fact that salvation comes through the Jews. This is the vision that Isaiah, the prophet, saw concerning Judah and Jerusalem:

> And it shall come to pass in the last days, that the mountain of the Lord's house shall be established in the top of the mountains [this refers to the temple that would be erected on Mount Zion], and shall be exalted above the hills; and all

nations shall flow unto it. And many people shall go and say, Come ye, and let us go up to the mountain of the Lord, to the house of the God of Jacob; and he will teach us of his ways, and we will walk in his paths: for out of Zion shall go forth the law, and the word of the Lord from Jerusalem. And he shall beat their sword into plowshares [this means that the nations shall convert their weapons into agricultural tools] and their spears into pruninghooks: nation shall not lift up sword against nation, neither shall they learn war anymore.

Isaiah 2:1–4

Finally, peace shall come to this earth after the Messiah (the Savior) is sent by the Creator God to save our world from complete destruction.

Yes, many people and strong nations shall come to seek the Lord of hosts in Jerusalem, and to pray before the Lord. Thus saith the Lord of hosts; in those days it shall come to pass, that ten men shall take hold out of all languages of the nations even shall take hold of the skirt of him that is a Jew, saying, We will go with you: for we have heard that God is with you.

After Armageddon, ten men from various nations (the number ten refers to a representative group) shall go up to Jerusalem in order to follow the Jews for guidance. All the nations and races are accepted and permitted in the house of God, as it is written: "Also the son of strangers shall join themselves to the Lord, to serve him and to love the name of the Lord, to be his servants, every one that keepeth the Sabbath from polluting it, and taketh hold of my covenant" (Isaiah 56:6).

After the great tribulation and the War of Armageddon, mankind will not learn war, nor will he attack one another; but all people and various races will go up to Jerusalem to learn the ways of God, which are just for everybody. The Israelites will play a major role in teaching the laws of God

to the various races; there will be no slavery, no persecution nor race prejudice. All people will be received with open arms, with sincere love and brotherhood. Peace at last! Peace at last!

Bibliography

Abramowitz, J. "The Negro in the Populist Movement." *Journal of Negro History* (July, 1953).

Aptheker, Herbert. *To Be Free: Studies in American Negro History*. New York: International Publishing Company, 1975.

Buck, Paul H. *The Road to Reunion*. Magnolia, Maryland: Peter Smith, Publisher, Inc. 1959.

Donald, Henderson H. *The Negro Freedman: Life Conditions of the American Negro in the Early Years after Emancipation*. Reprint of 1952 edition. New York: Cooper Square, Publishers, Inc., 1971.

Douglass, Frederick. *The Life and Writings of Frederick Douglass*. Edited by Phillip S. Foner. New York: International Publishing Company, 1975.

Du Bois, W.E. *Black Reconstruction in America, 1860–1880*. New York: Russell and Russell, Publishers, 1962.

Du Bois, W.E. *The Souls of Black Folk*. New York: Washington Square Press, Inc., 1970.

Franklin, John H., ed. *From Slavery to Freedom: A History of American Negroes*. 4th ed. New York: Alfred A. Knopf, Inc., 1974.

Hacker, Louis M. *The Triumph of American Capitalism*. New York: Columbia University Press, 1940.

Hicks, John D. *The Populist Revolt: A History of the Farmers Alliance and the People's Party*. Lincoln, Nebraska: University of Nebraska Press, 1961.

Lincoln, Eric. *The Negro Pilgrimage in America*. New York: Bantam Books, 1961.

Mannix, Daniel. *Black Cargo*. New York: Viking Press, 1962.

Marx, Karl. *Capital*. Edited by Frederick Engels. 3 vols. Fairfield, New Jersey: International Publishing Company, 1937.

Matison, S.E. *Journal of Negro History* (October, 1948).

Myers, William S. *The Republican Party: A History*. Reprint of 1928 edition. New York: Johnson Reprint Corporation, 1968.

Parrington, Vernon L. *Main Currents in American Thought*, vol. II, *The Romantic Revolution in America, 1800–1860*. New York: Harcourt Brace Jovanovich, Inc., 1955.

Powderly, Terence V. *Thirty Years of Life & Labor*, rev. ed. Fairfield, New Jersey: Augustus M. Kelley, Pubs., 1940.

Redding, J. Saunders. *They Came in Chains*, rev. ed. Philadelphia, Pennsyl-

vania: J.B. Lippincott Company, 1973.

Todes, Charlotte. *William H. Sylvis and the National Labor Union*. Reprint of 1942 edition. Westport, Connecticut: Hyperion Press, Inc., 1975.

Wesley, Charles H. *Negro Labor in the United States, 1850–1925: A Study in American Economic History*. Reprint of 1927 edition. New York: Russell and Russell Publishers, 1967.

Windsor Golden Series

P.O Box 310393   Phone: 770-969-2293
Atlanta GA 31131-0393   Email: windsorgs@bellsouth.net   Fax: 770-969-5677

Lectures by the Author

<u>Audio Cassette Tapes</u>

The Bible an African Book: Resurrection of the Dry Bones (30 min.)	$ 7.00
Prophecies of the Nations Coming to Jerusalem (30 min)	$ 7.00
Paganism in the Ancient World (30 min)	$ 7.00
The One God Concept (30 min)	$ 7.00
New Testament Analyzed (approx 45 min.)	$10.00
Historical Background of Jesus (60 min)	$10.00
Beginner's Hebrew Language (4 cassette tapes & workbooks)	$65.00
Advanced Hebrew Language (4 cassette tapes & workbooks)	$65.00

<u>Videos</u>

The Ethiopian Jews (the black Jews of Ethiopia and their immigration to Israel) (22 min Part1) (The Confession of a white Jew about the Ethiopian Jews and the messiah) (22 min Part II) $15.00

Lost Identity (The history of the ancient black civilization and the black Hebrews) (60 min.) $20.00

Whoever You Thought You Were..You're A Jew (The history of the black Hebrews in Spain and the black Moors) (45 min.) $15.00

<u>Books</u>

From Babylon to Timbuktu (by Prof Rudolph R. Windsor) (The history of the ancient races including the black Hebrews) $11.95

The Valley of the Dry Bones (by Prof. Rudolph R. Windsor) (The conditions that face black people in America) $10.95

When Is the Next War? (by Professor R Windsor (Biblical and psychic prophecies for our time) $12.95

Judea Trembles under Rome (by Prof. Rudolph R. Windsor)
(Greek and Roman persecution of the black Hebrews) $11.95

Deborah and Barak (by Prof. Rudolph R. & Mary L. Windsor)
(A historical, piece about the fight for freedom from Canaanite
oppression and the development of spirituality in ancient Israel) $12.95

The Complete Hebrew Bible
In English and Hebrew with commentaries, 25 sketches, charts
and maps with a total of 2,079 pages (hard cover) $60.00

The New Complete Works of Josephus
Antiquity of the Hebrews and Judean wars, Josephus' polemics with
Apion; photos, tables and charts; and index and commentaries
(soft cover with 1,144 pages) $35.00

The Essential Works of Josephus
The history of the black Hebrews from the beginning of their
history to the time of the Romans. Has charts and maps, with
415 pages, (hard cover) $30.00

Method of Payment

Send check and/or money order made payable to:

Windsor Golden Series
P.O. Box 310393
Atlanta, GA 31131-0393

VISA, MASTER CARD, & DISCOVER credit cards welcomed

UPS
Please send $6.50 shipping & handling for each item. For each
additional item, send $.50 more.

United States Postal Service
Please send $1.42 for each item, and $.50 for each additional item.

Do You Need Financing for Any of the Following:

Home or **Business**

- To Purchase your home
  or
- To Refinance Your Existing Home
  Or
- To Consolidate Your Debt

- To Get the Equity from Your Home

No Credit! Low Credit Score! NO PROBLEM!

Let NLC of Georgia, Inc. Help You Obtain the Finances for That Project!

We are located in 46 states including Hawaii & Puerto Rico

For information, contact: **Mary L. Windsor**, Mortgage Specialist

3490 Shallowford Road, Suite 300, Chamblee, GA 30341
Phone: 770-969-1627; Cell: 404-513-2586, Fax: 770-969-5677
Email: windsorgs@bellsouth.net
Website: www.mynlc.com

Become a loan originator and make money while helping others.

Service with Integrity

YTB

Your Travel Biz
www.ytbnet.com/wgstravel

Have you dreamed of traveling to exotic places but felt that you couldn't because you thought it was too expensive for you?

Well! DREAMS <u>DO</u> come true!

How would you like to fly within the continental USA for $55.00 one way, book cruises, stay at 5 star hotels, rent cars for less, and more exciting opportunities? All this for pennies on the dollar. For details, call:

Mary L. Windsor @ 770-969-1627

By the way, you can travel and earn a supplemental income.

Call 1-888-619-9074 and listen to a 3-minute tape.

Airfare   Rental Cars   Cruises

Vacation Packages   Hotels

Biography

RUDOLPH R. WINDSOR, a native of New Jersey, settled in Philadelphia, where he attended Community College, studying Psychology and Political Science; Gratz College, where he majored in Hebraic Studies; and Temple University, where he majored in Middle Eastern Studies. He received his B.H.L. degree in 1978. He says of his book, "My motive in writing it was to give the true history of the Afro-American, which has been suppressed and excluded from American textbooks. Moreover, the books that had been written on the Afro-American were grossly distorted and filled with misinterpretations and race prejudice. I was convinced that only when more Afro-Americans and liberals begin to write history, would more truth be revealed." The author realizes that the current educators shouldn't be blamed for these conditions because they only inherit them from previous generations.

Mr. Windsor loves children and has four sons and one daughter. Professor Windsor is the author of the book: From Babylon to The Timbuktu.

The Valley of
the Dry Bones